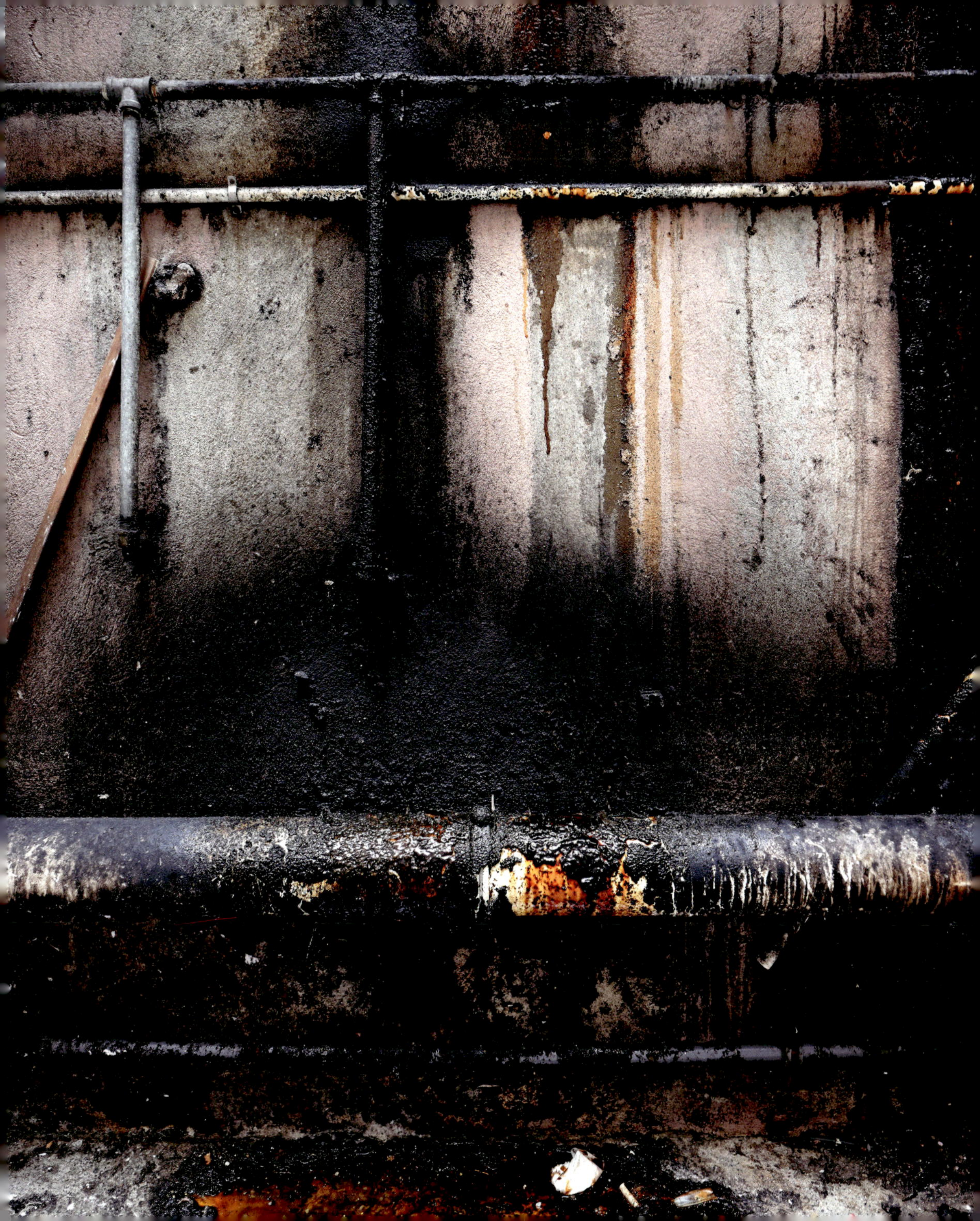

**KERBER** PHOTO

**KERBER** PHOTO

# Metropolis Sunday

HONG KONG SERIES

Matthias Forster

## Metropolis Sunday

*Metropolis Sunday* takes the viewer on a journey behind the skyscrapers' gleaming fronts to discover the light in the dark, the beautiful in the ugly and the virtuoso in the banal. Metropolis, the mother city, is the epitome of the cosmopolitan city. Sunday is the day of rest. *Metropolis Sunday* is an alternative concept to the hectic, stimulus-flooded society. Away from the noisy, busy streets, the city is supplied with energy, food and people. Contrary to the cliché of the noisy and overcrowded metropolis, the reverse side reveals almost deserted and quiet places. This is where the city catches its breath and comes to rest, where space and time recede into the background. The rear of the skyscraper formation can be seen as a reflection of society; on the prestigious front, many things are presented beautifully and neatly. Away from the usual ideal of beauty, the informal and improvised reveals itself as an atmospheric backdrop in its own right.

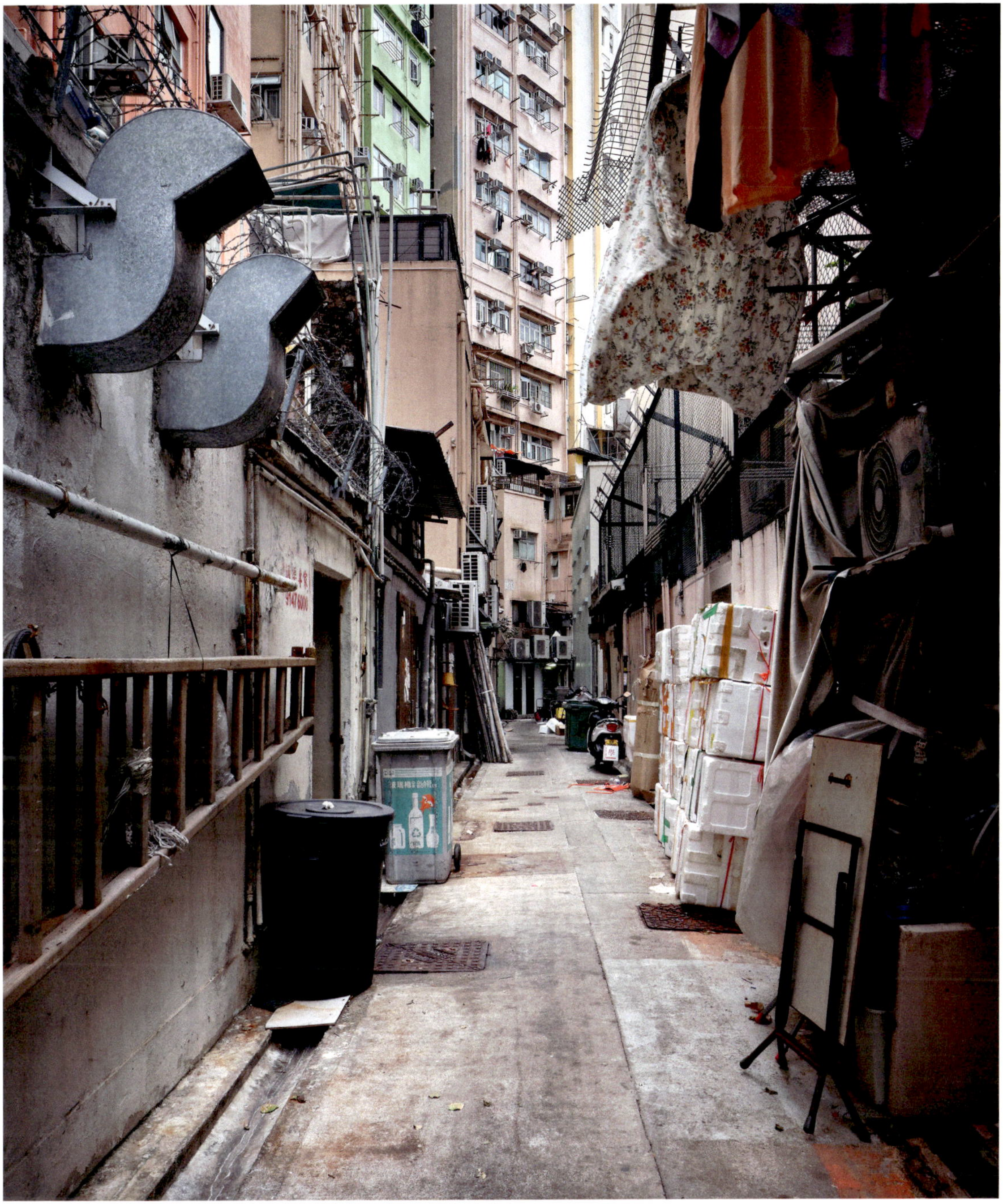

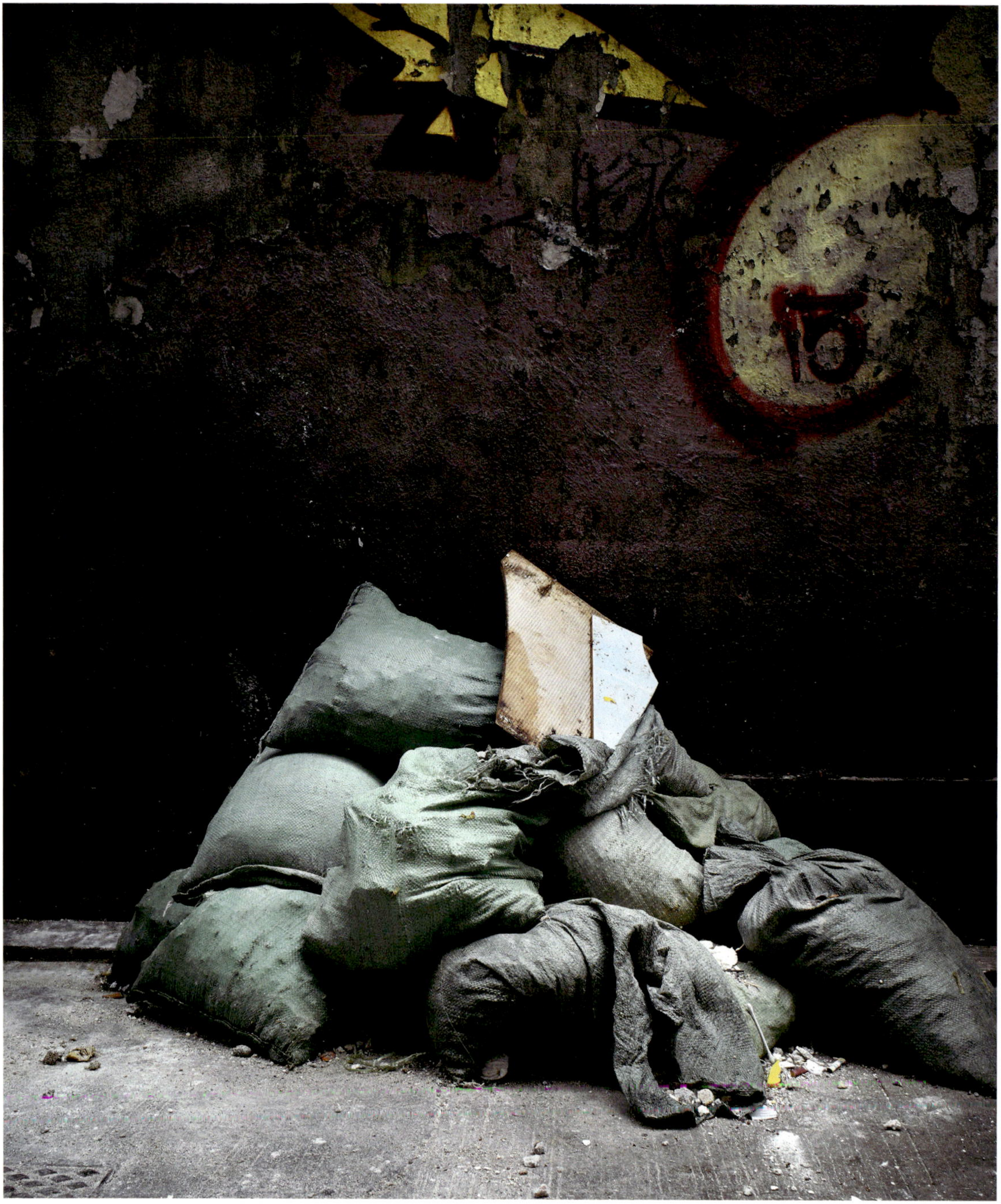

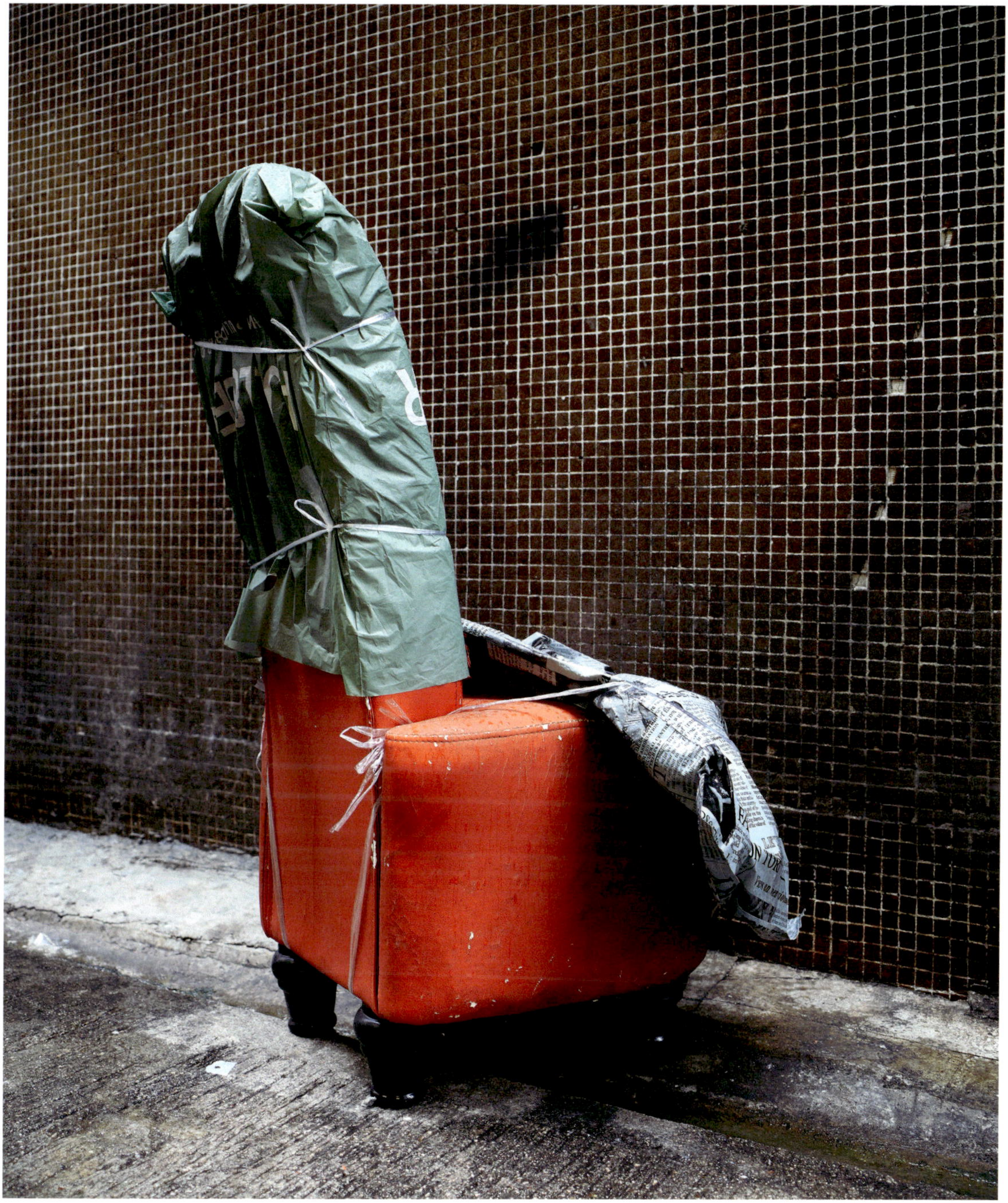

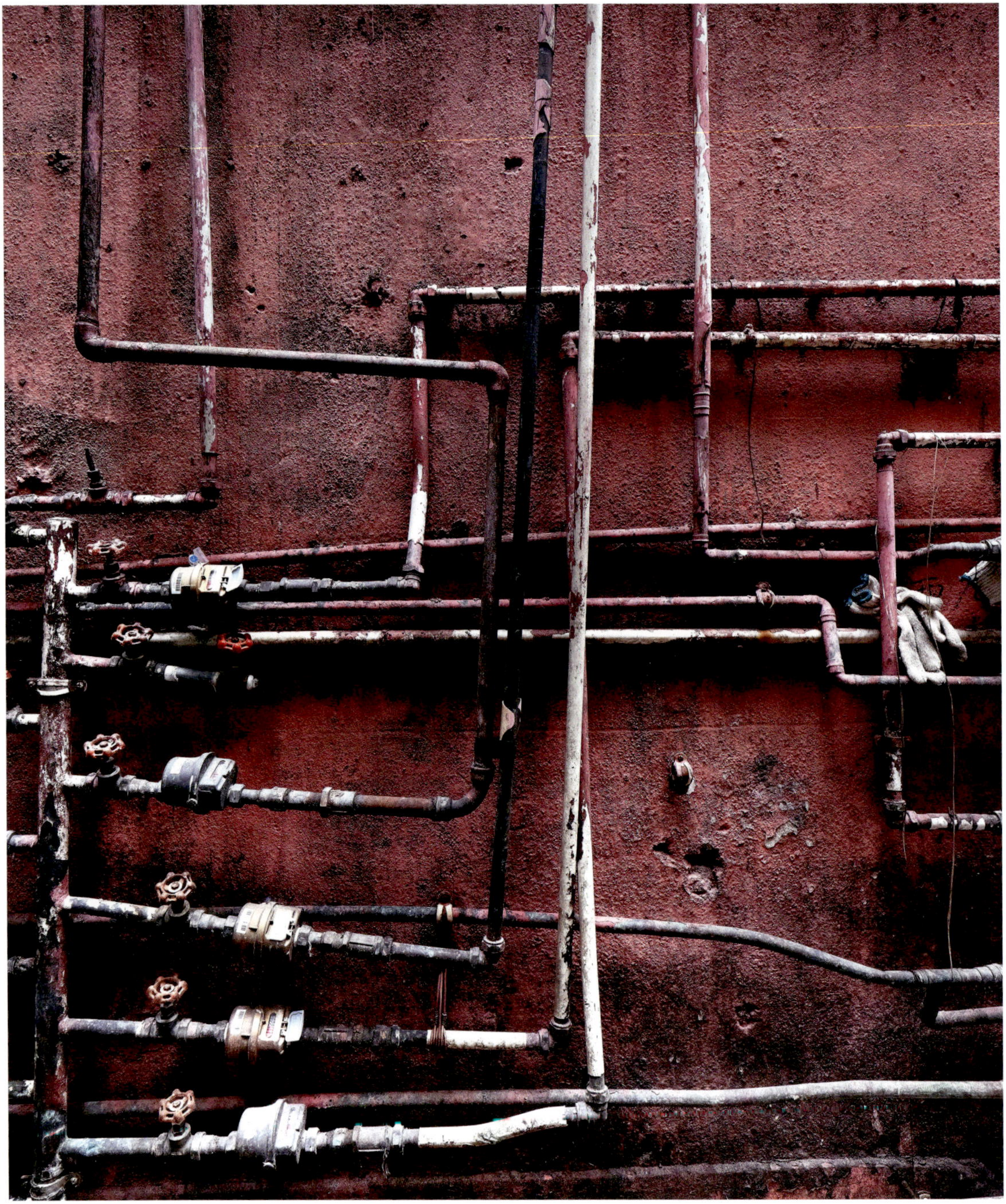

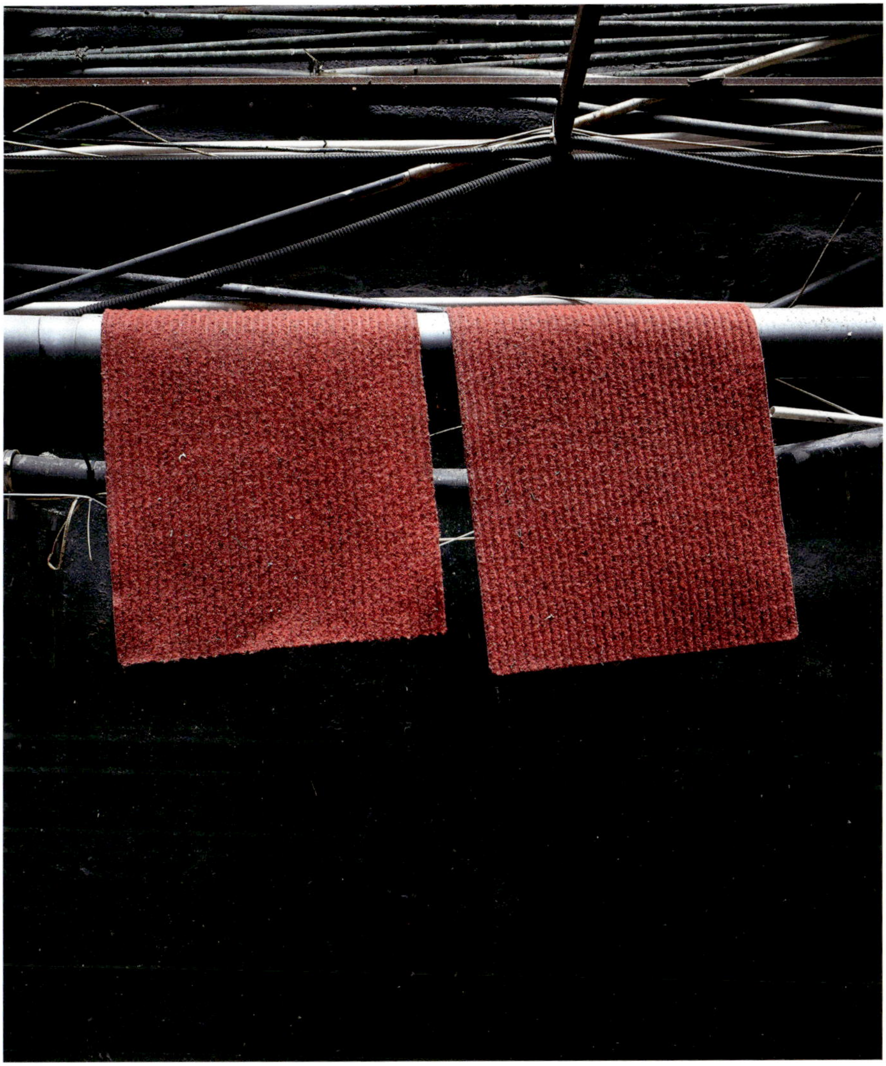

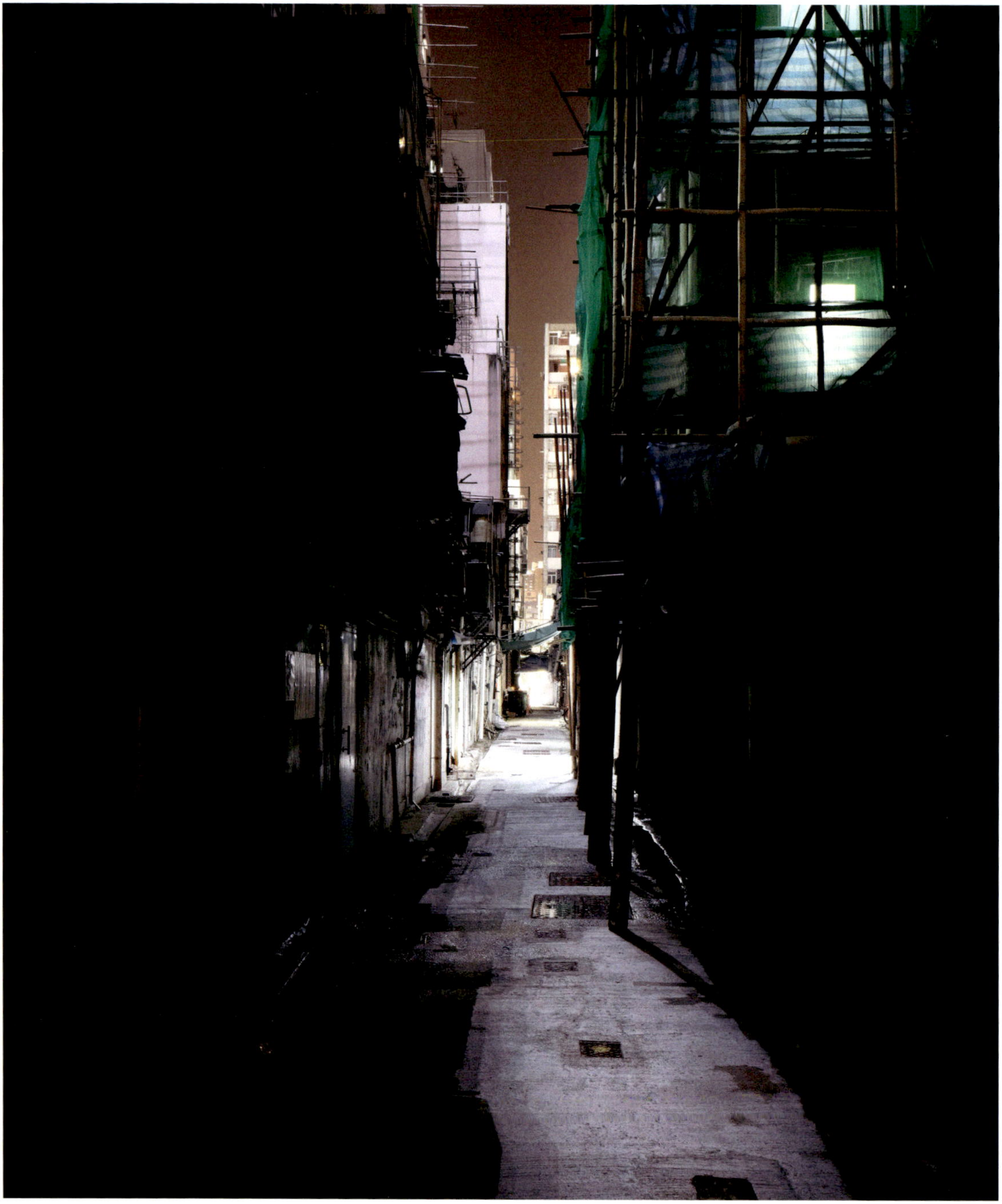

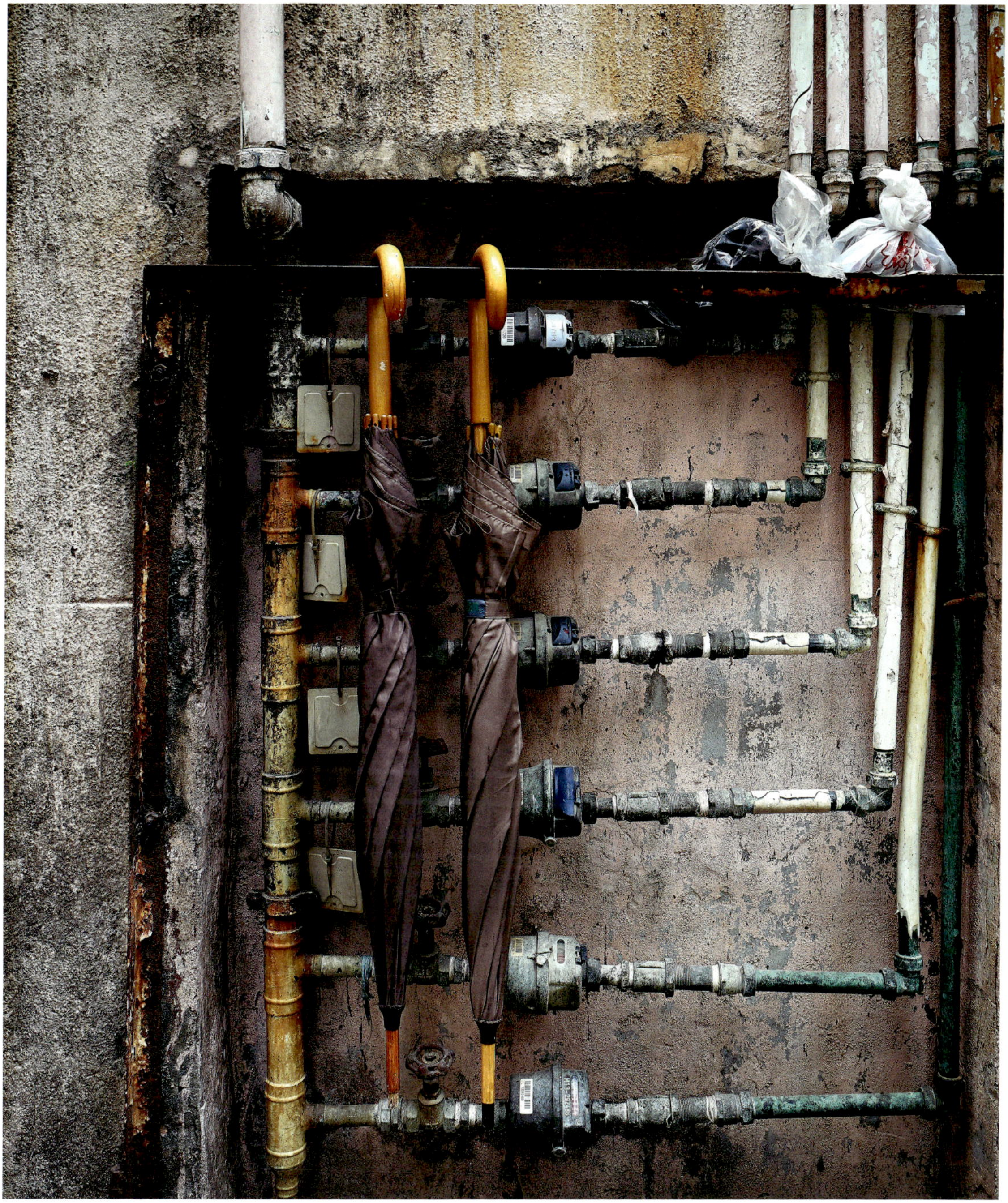

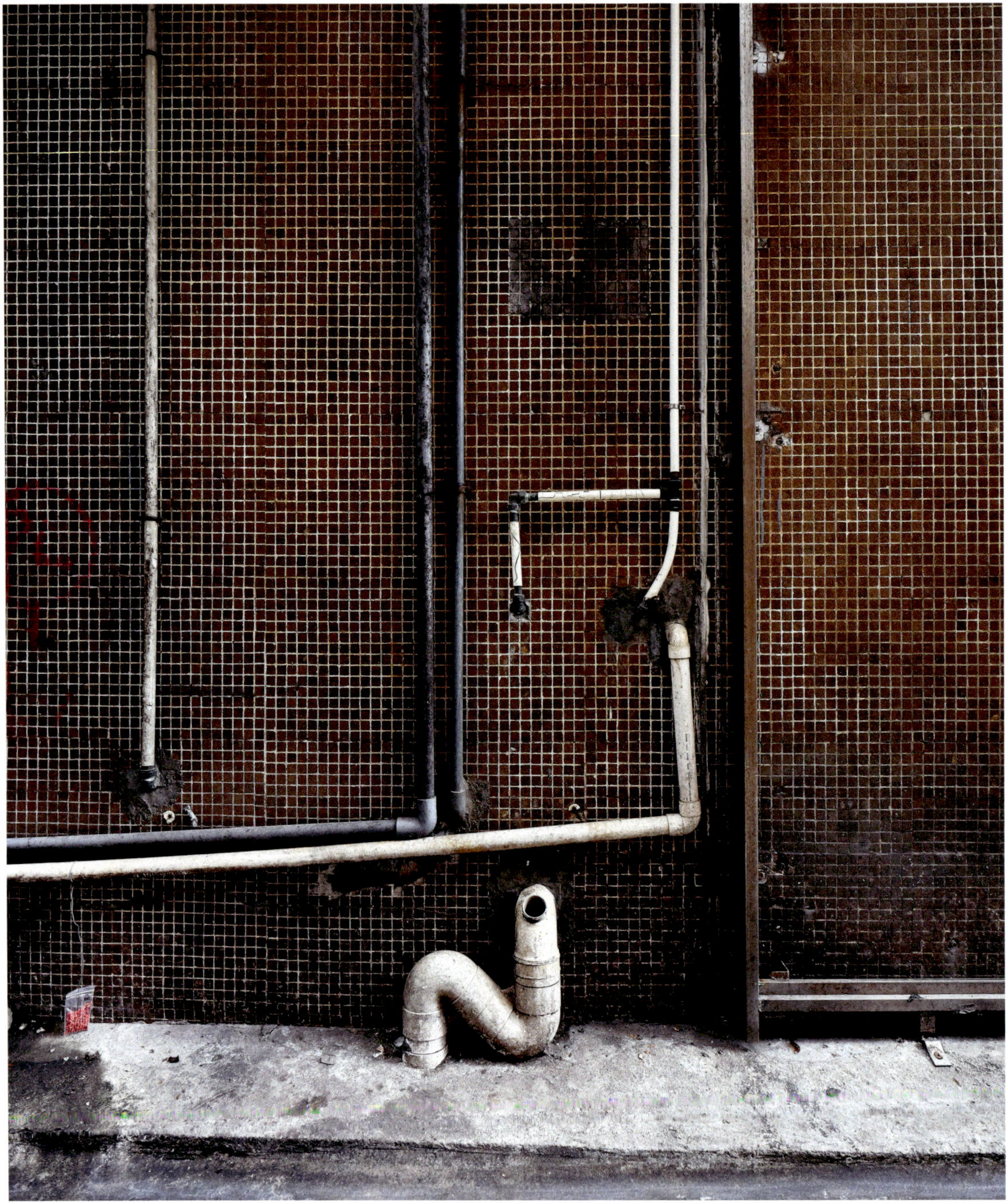

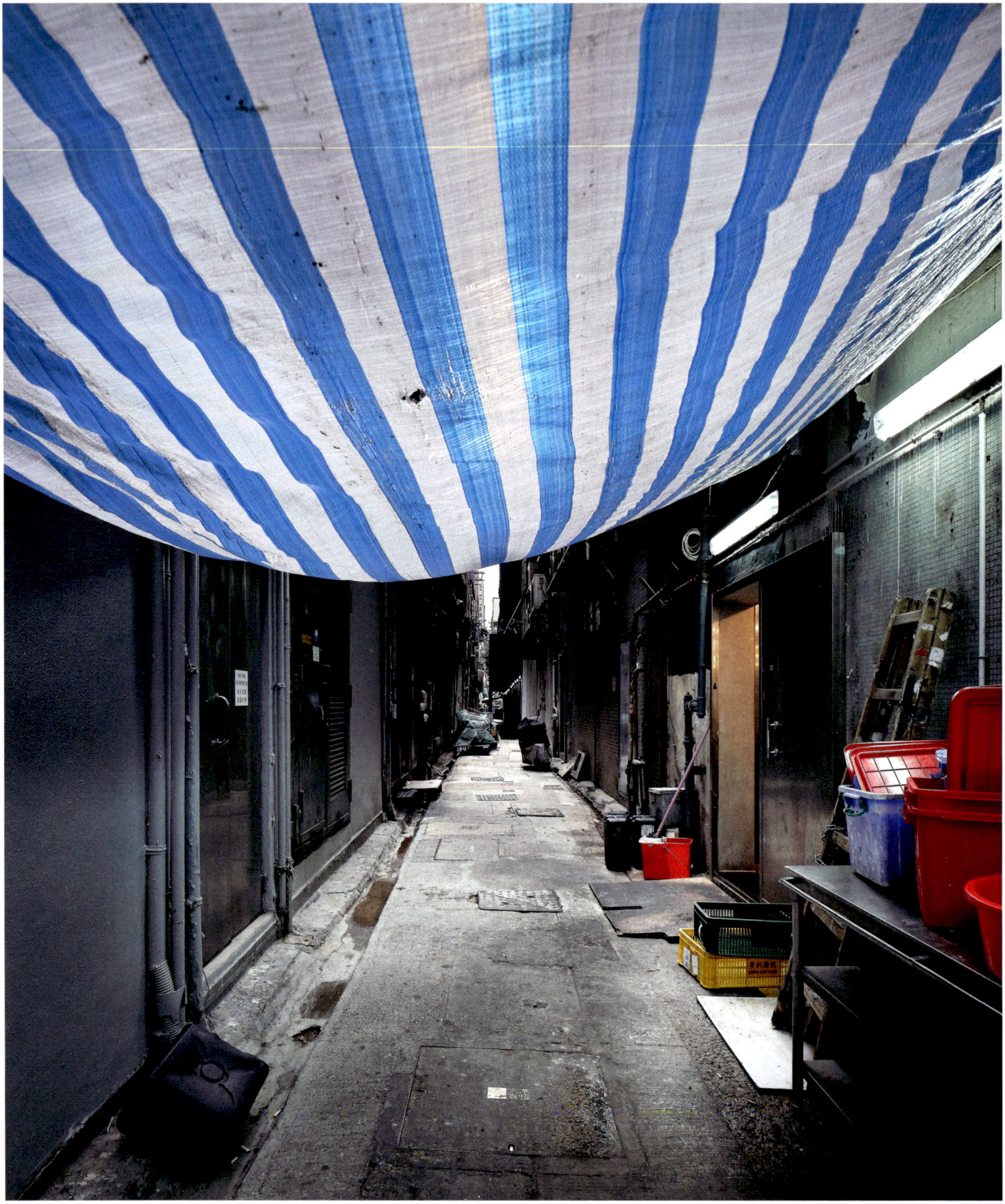

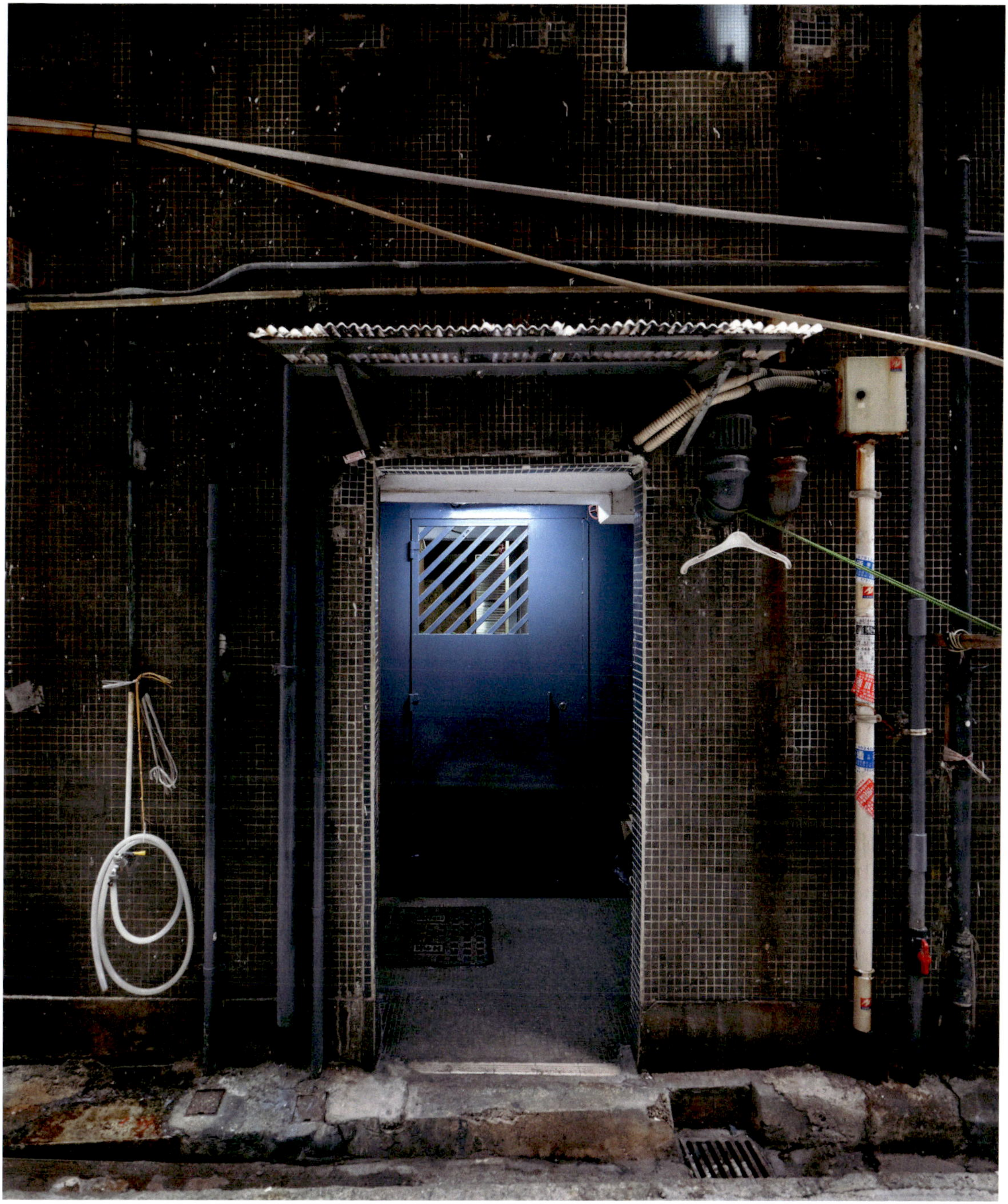

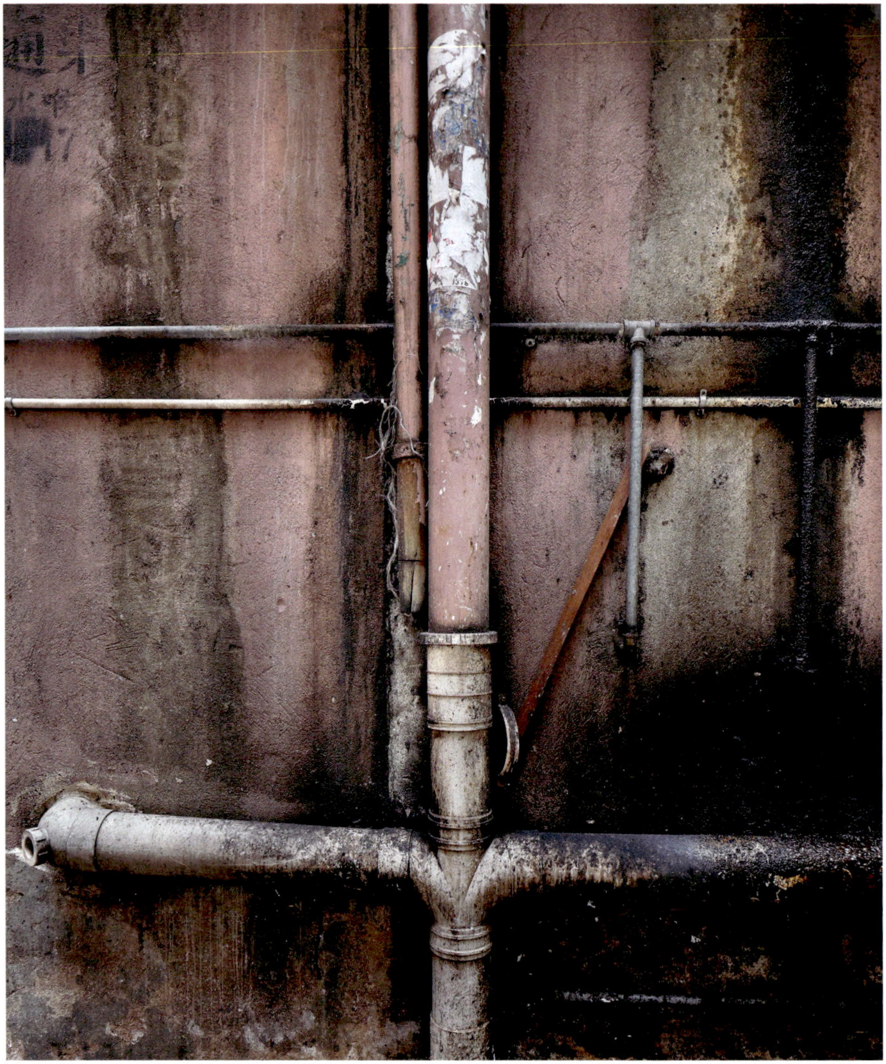

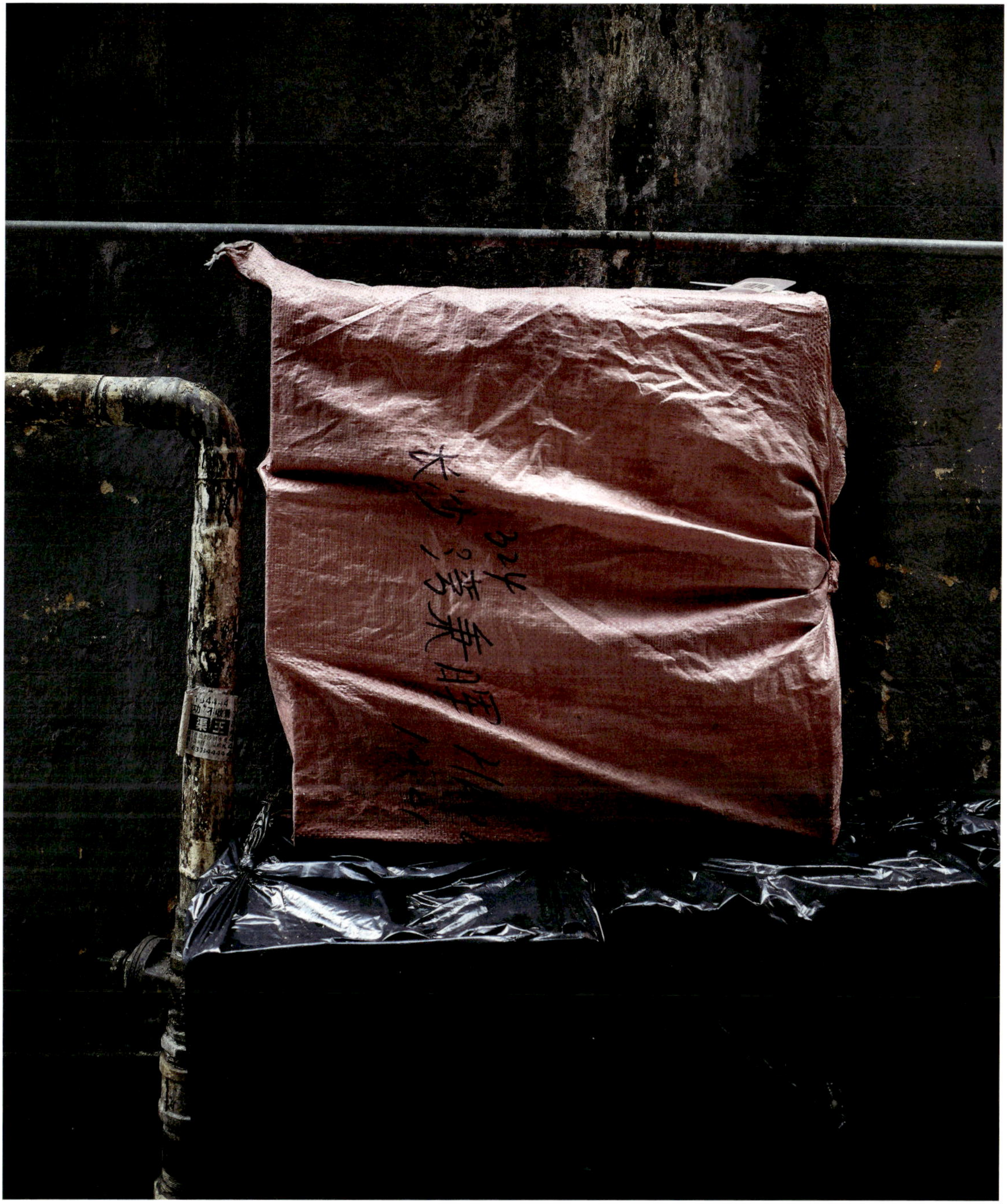

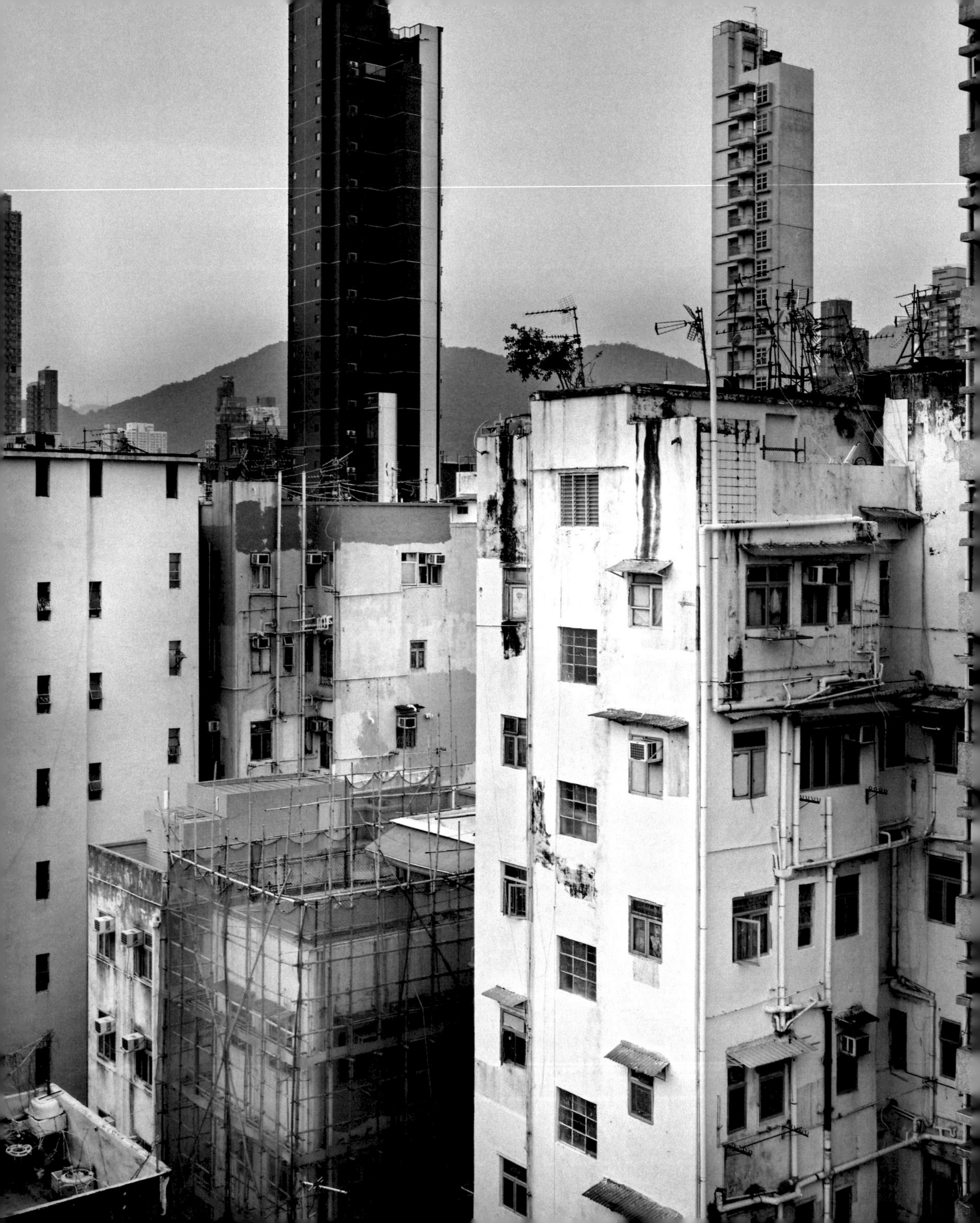

## 早 Morning

The unmistakable sound of that creaky lock, its iron door opening. At 9.30 sharp the woman descends with the man, both are well into their seventies.

They unload fifteen floors of residential trash bins excreted from the tower, save what's sellable, dispose of the rest.

Two large straw baskets on an industrial metal trolley, two folding chairs stored between the wall and the countless water pipes climbing up on the building's back, all the way into whose home. And an old battery powered radio.

I am the uninvited witness of this elaborately performed daily rite, their undisclosed bond meticulously expressed.

On their morning chirping sound I have relied for more than one decade. I must come out between 9.38 and 9.48 to feel the warmth of light, it is the only time our back lane is blessed with direct sun.

The celestial body's alignment lights and warms us three in a brief, precious, theatrical instant that is already lost in the folds of this city's unconscious.

Fleeting instants turn permanent in front of Matthias's lens. Traces of humanity evoke glimpses of his intended subjects' lifetimes and summon memories from the viewers' senses, tricking us into thinking those instants were left behind by our own existence. This angle masterfully makes the strange familiar, and the familiar strange in a never ending loop.

Without uttering a word, through the years they have offered me every object I have shown interest in, their generous basket materialising unpredictable leftover treasures from the innumerable floors above. The couple asks for nothing in return, ever, prompting me to do the same.

A gift based, wordless kinship chants of a generation of selfless survivors of flawless effectiveness. Instants predating our obstinacy with affirming constructed identities, silently grounding our desire for individuality indefinitely.

Their passage is otherwise made invisible throughout the following twenty-four hours, symptom of a city that has not chosen the human factor as its ethos.

Scouting humanity as it thrives in the shadow of modernity, Matthias offers the mundane, he is a flâneur in search of those elemental materials that make up history.

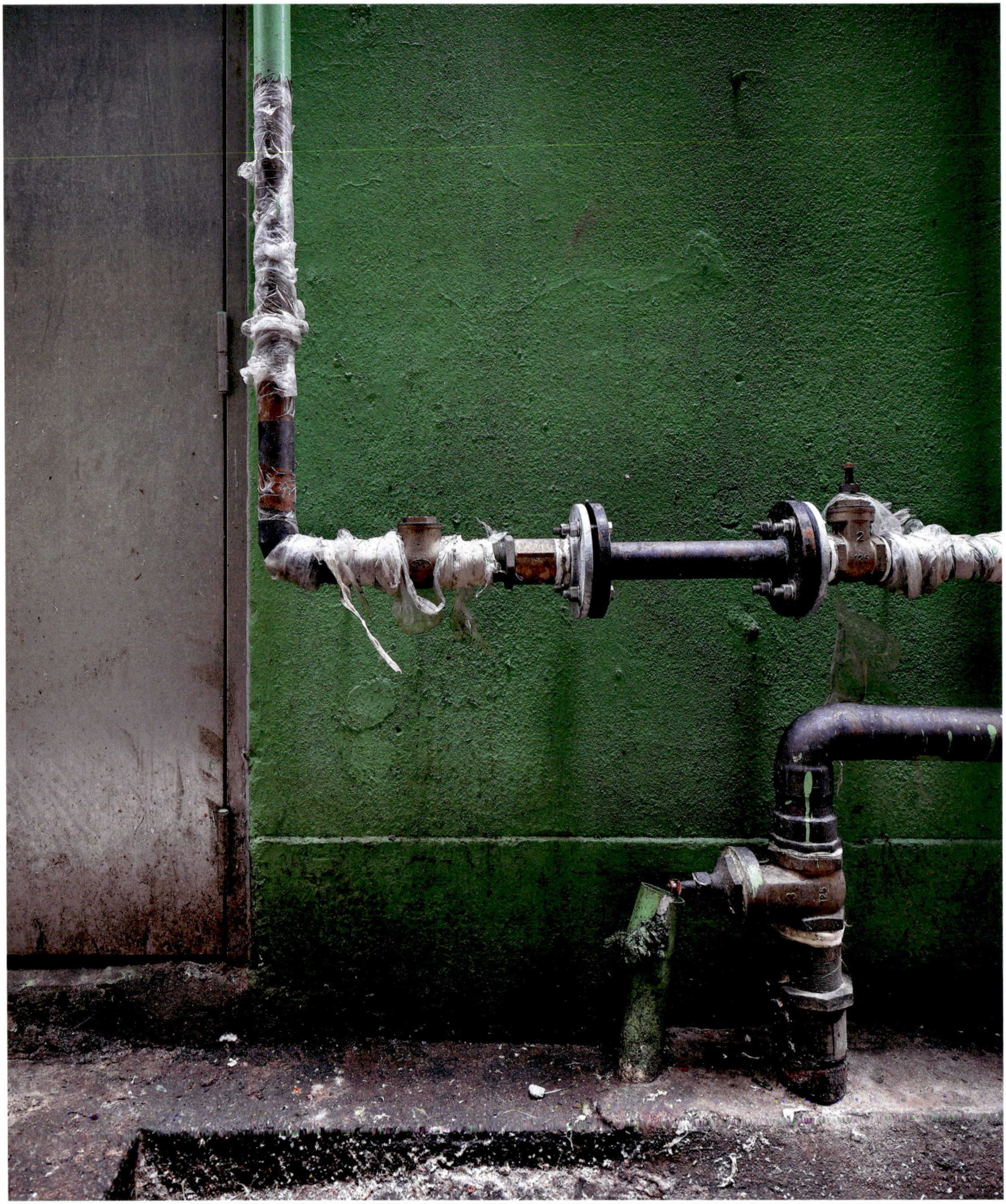

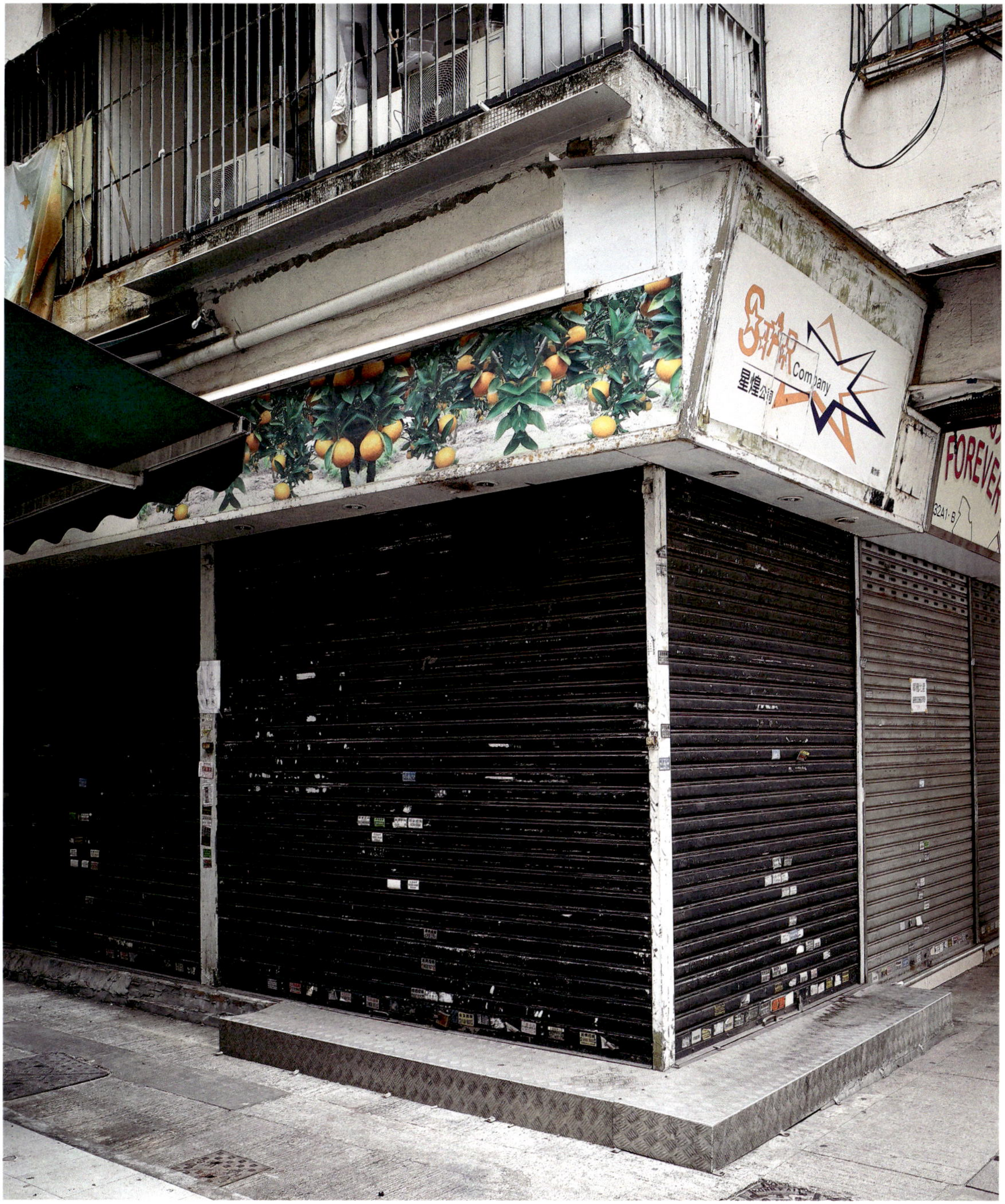
Company
星煌公司
FOREVER

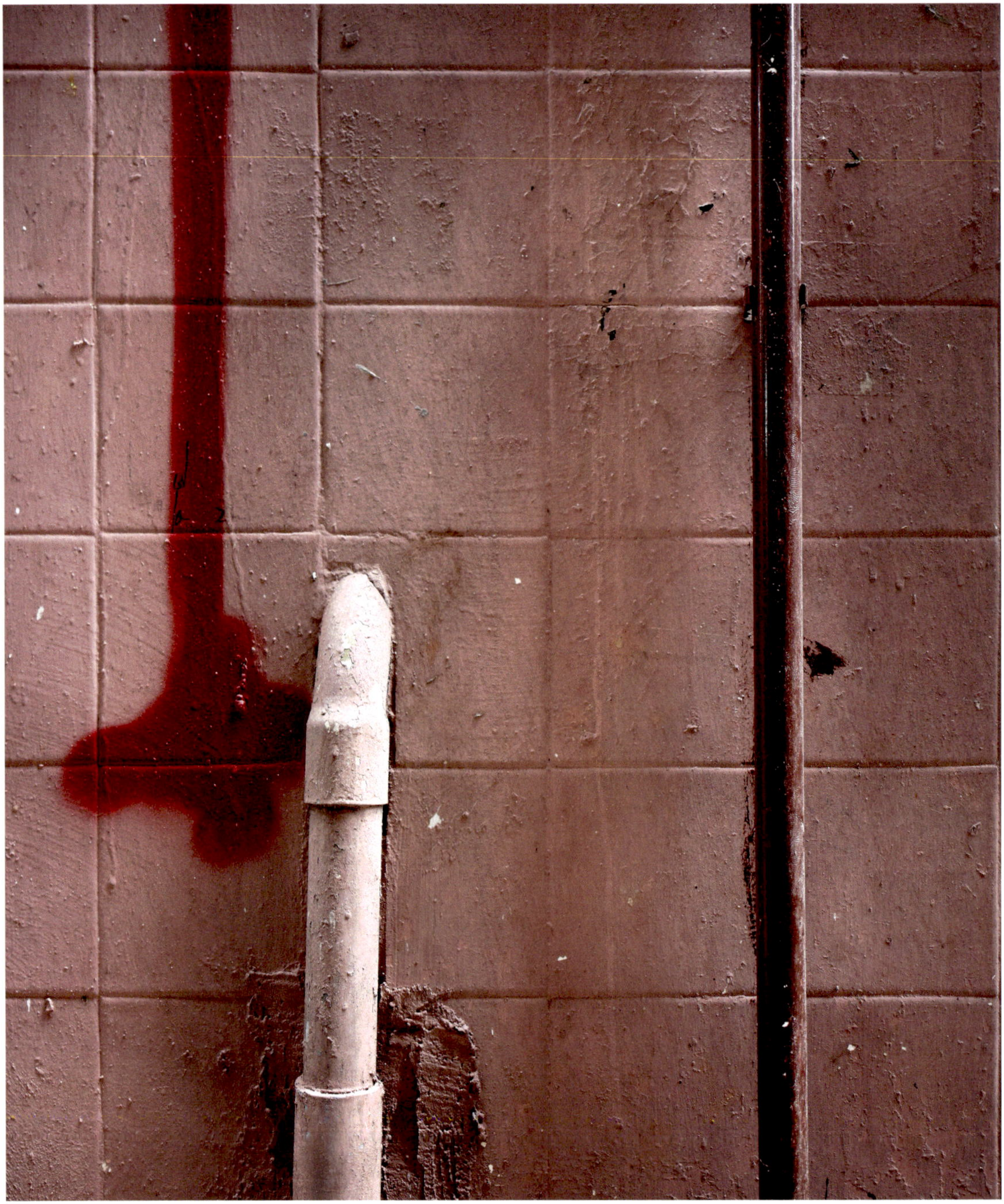

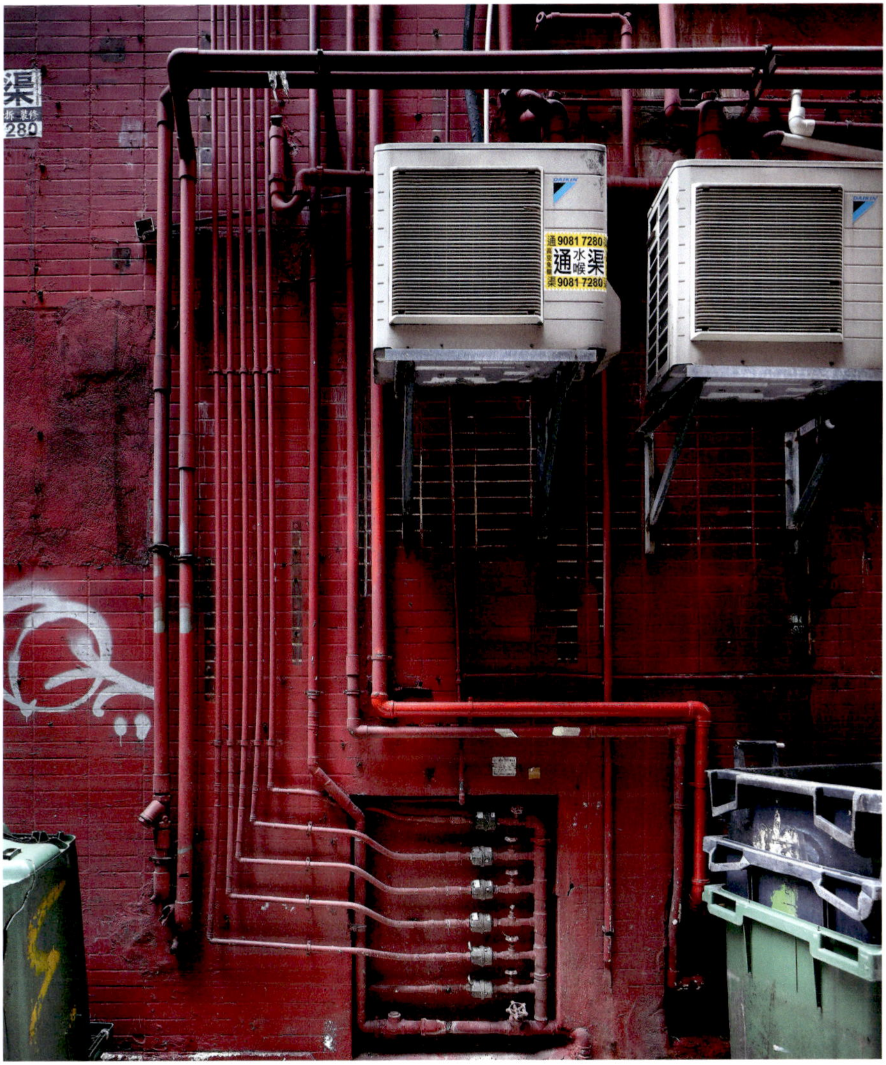
渠
拆 裝修
280
DAIKIN
通 9081 7280
通 水喉 渠
渠 9081 7280

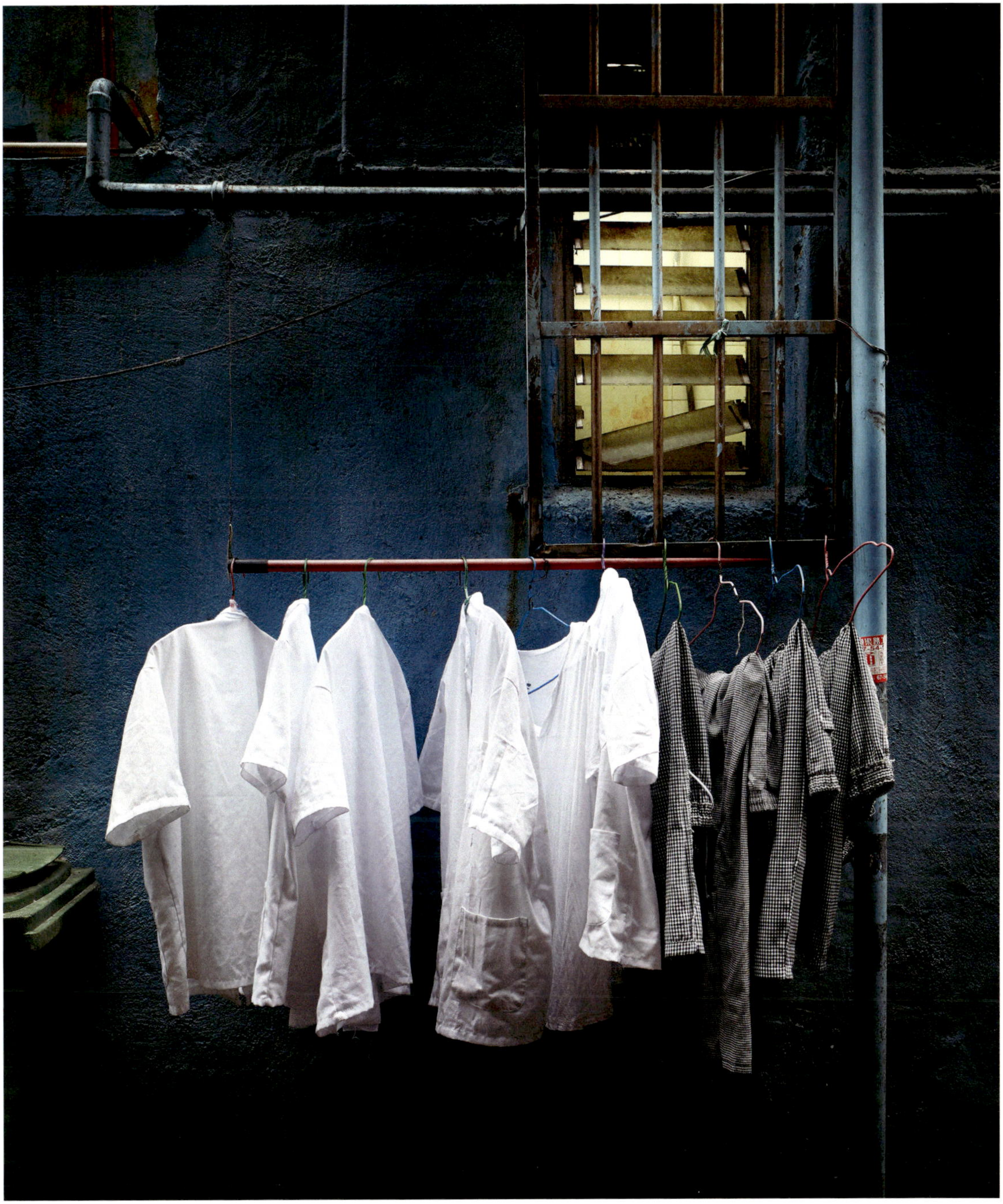

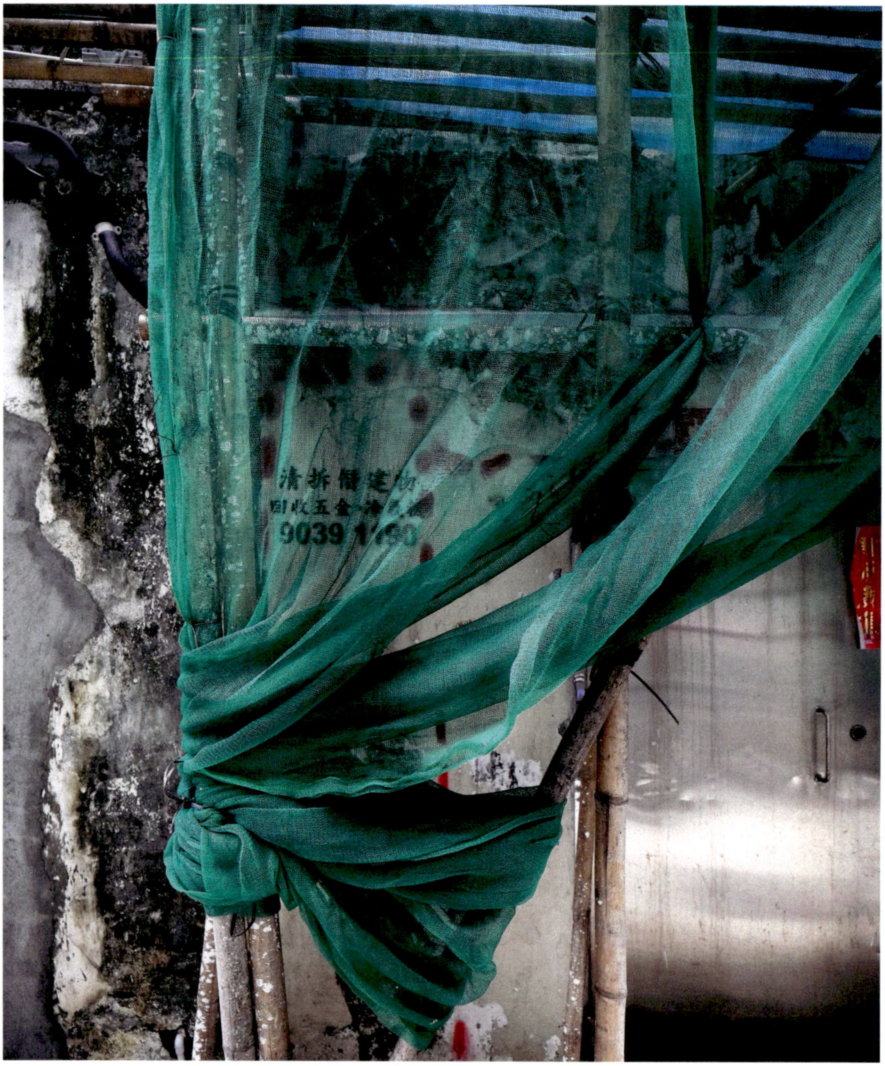
清拆僭建物

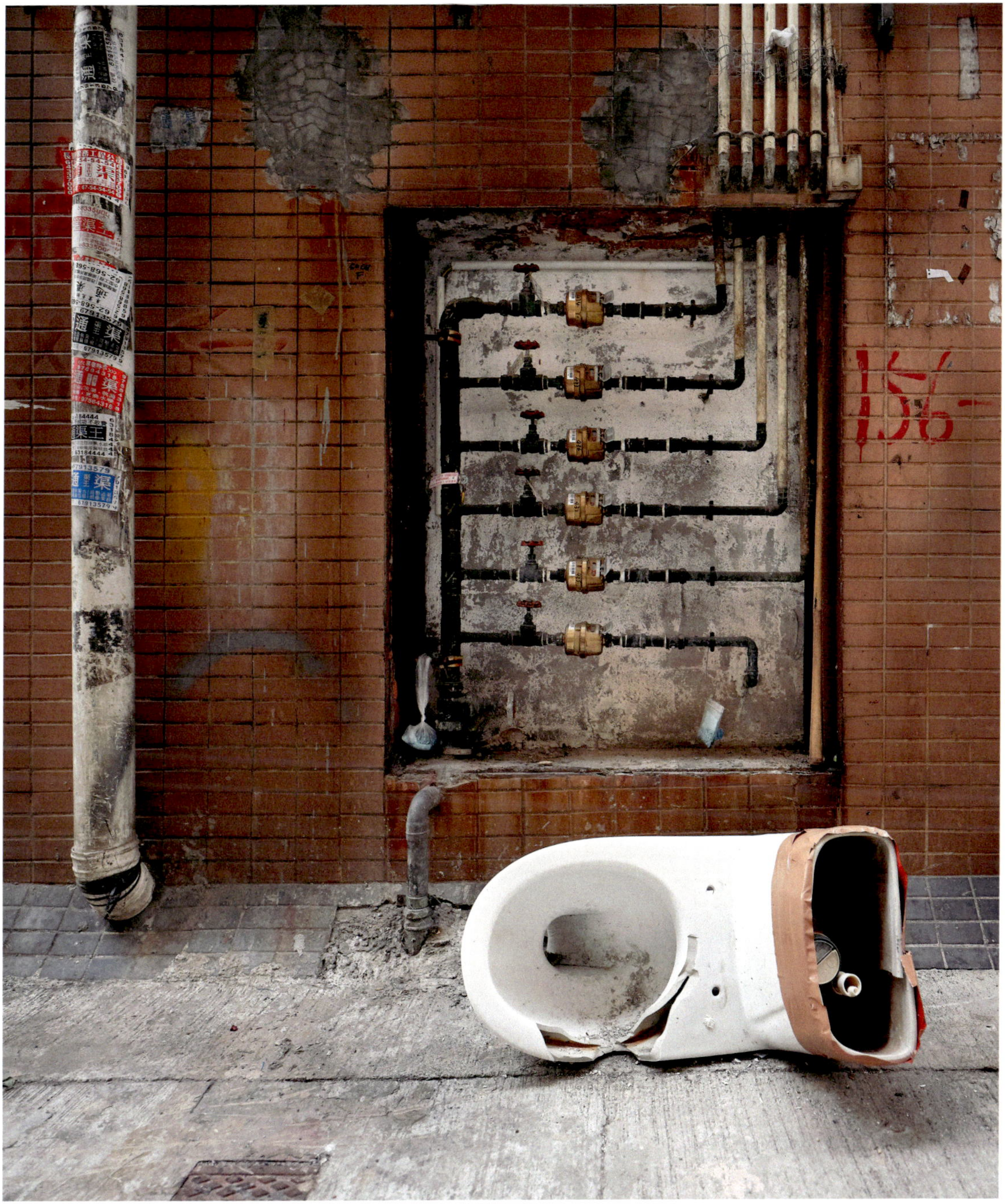
通渠
156

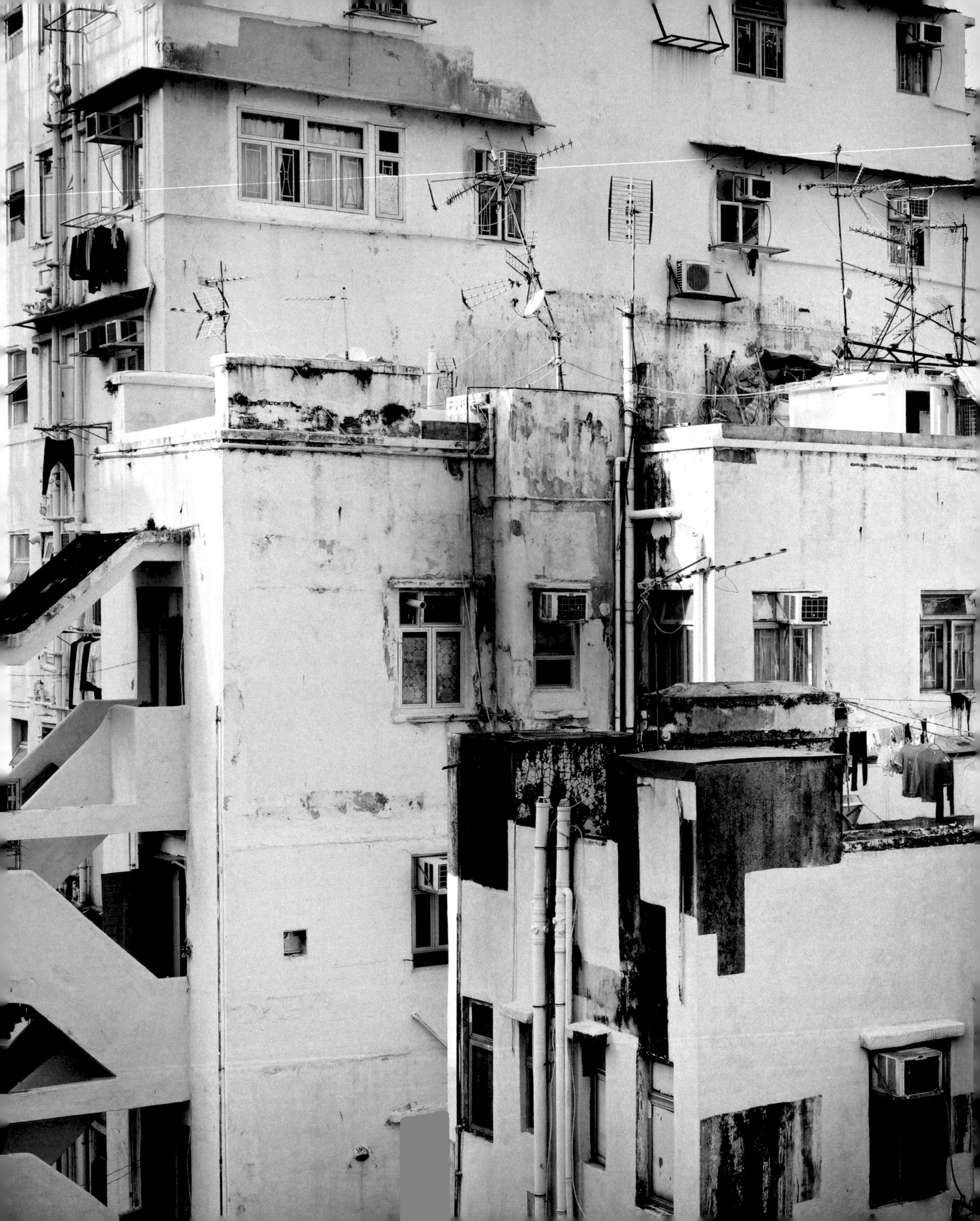

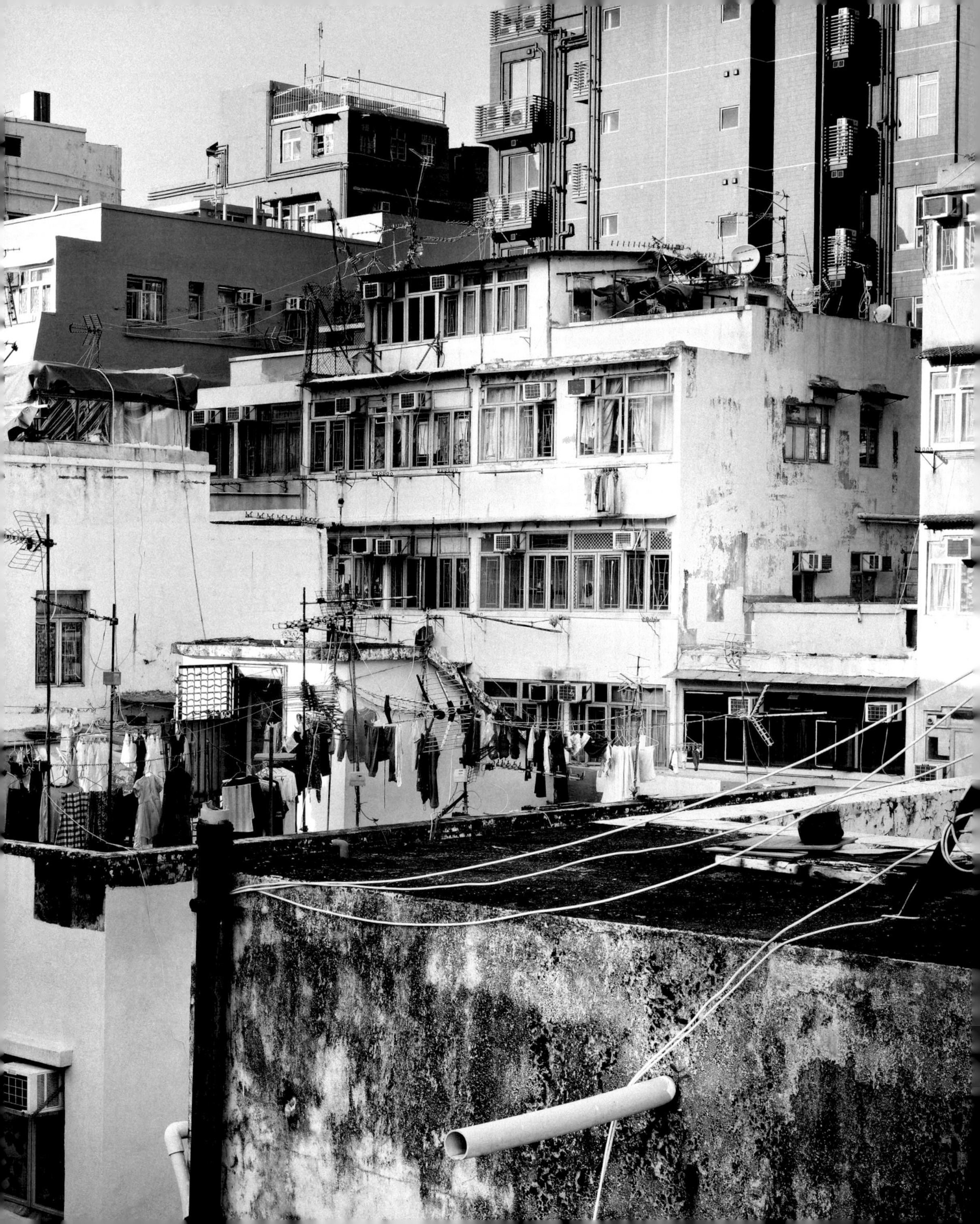

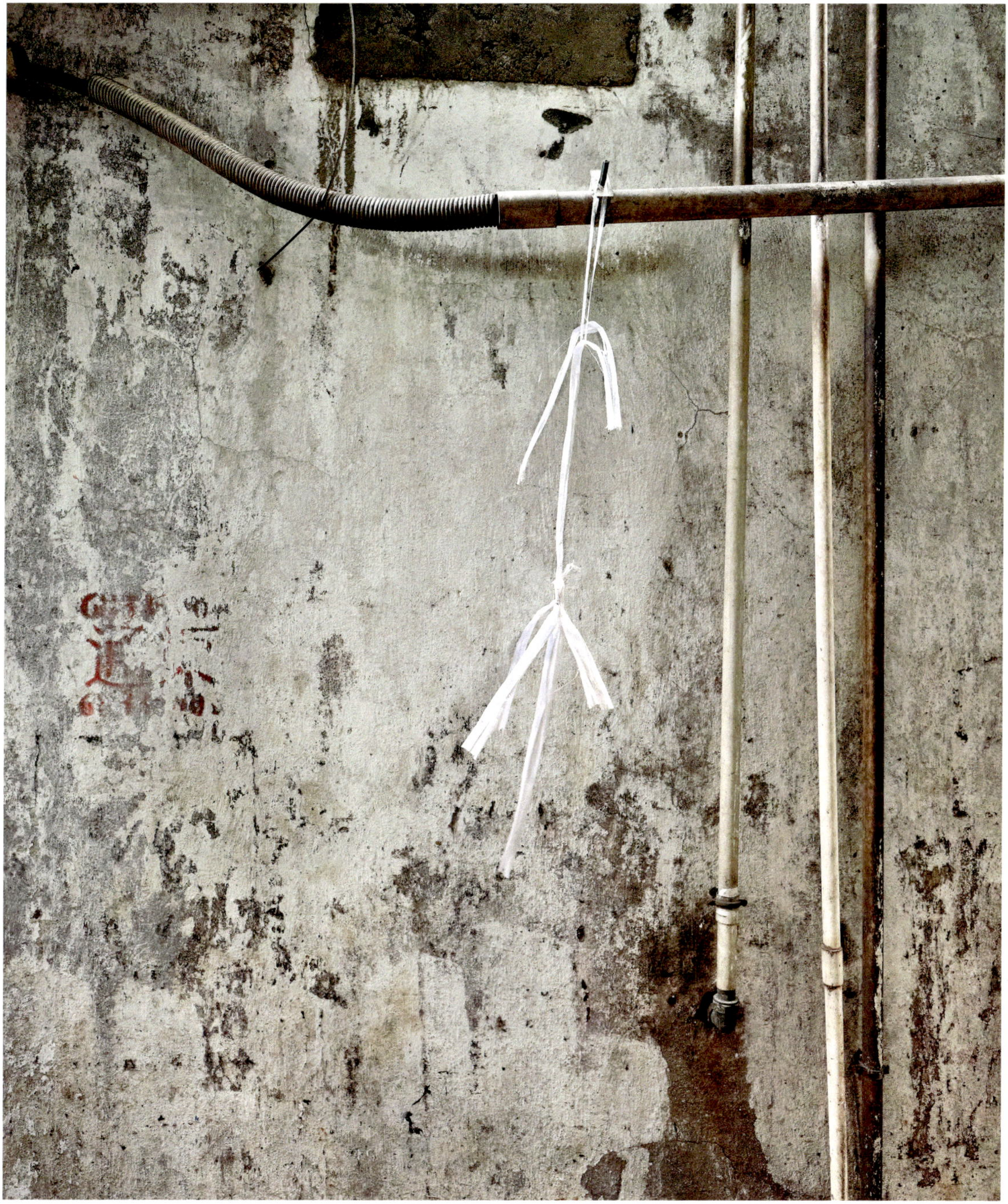

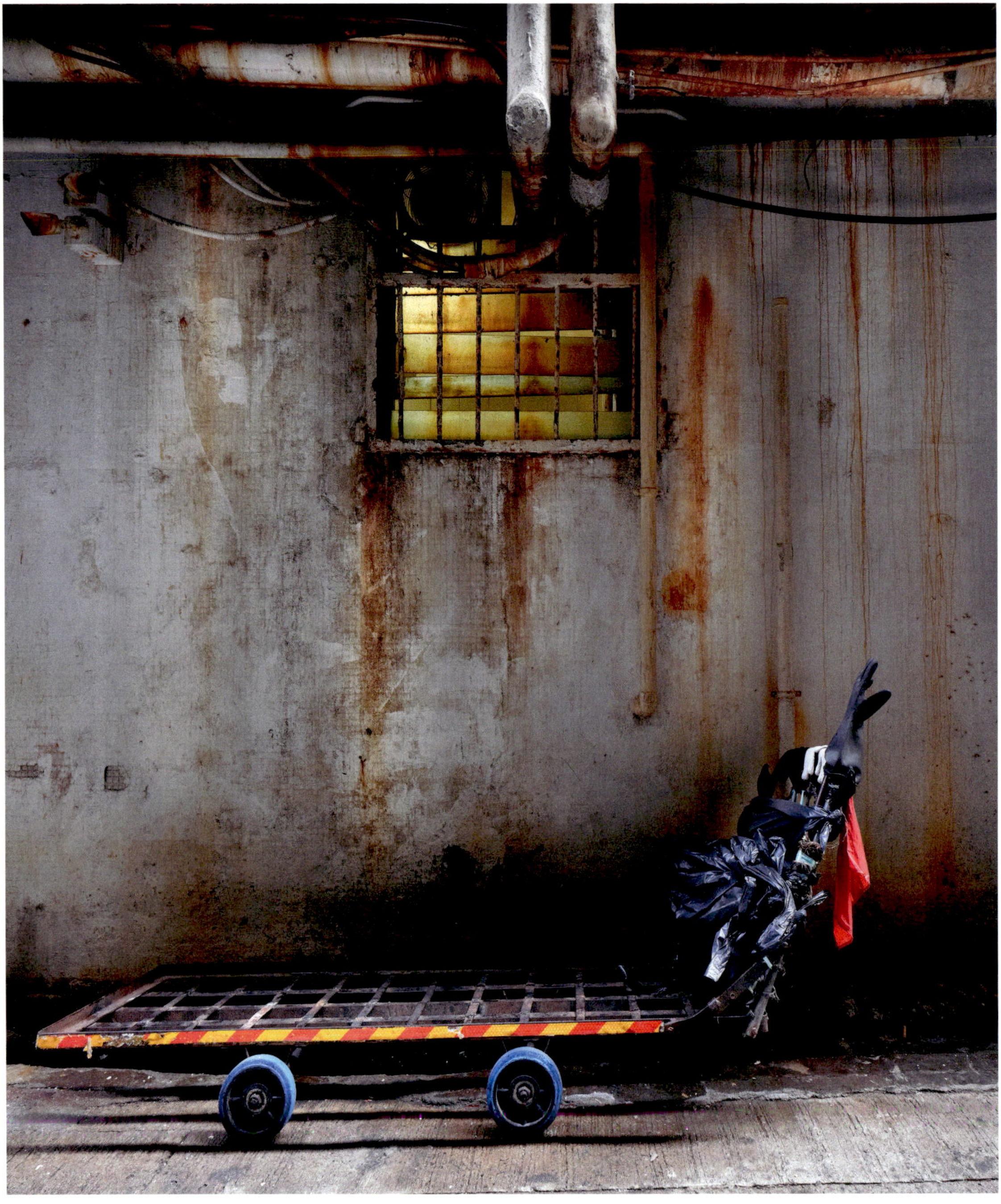

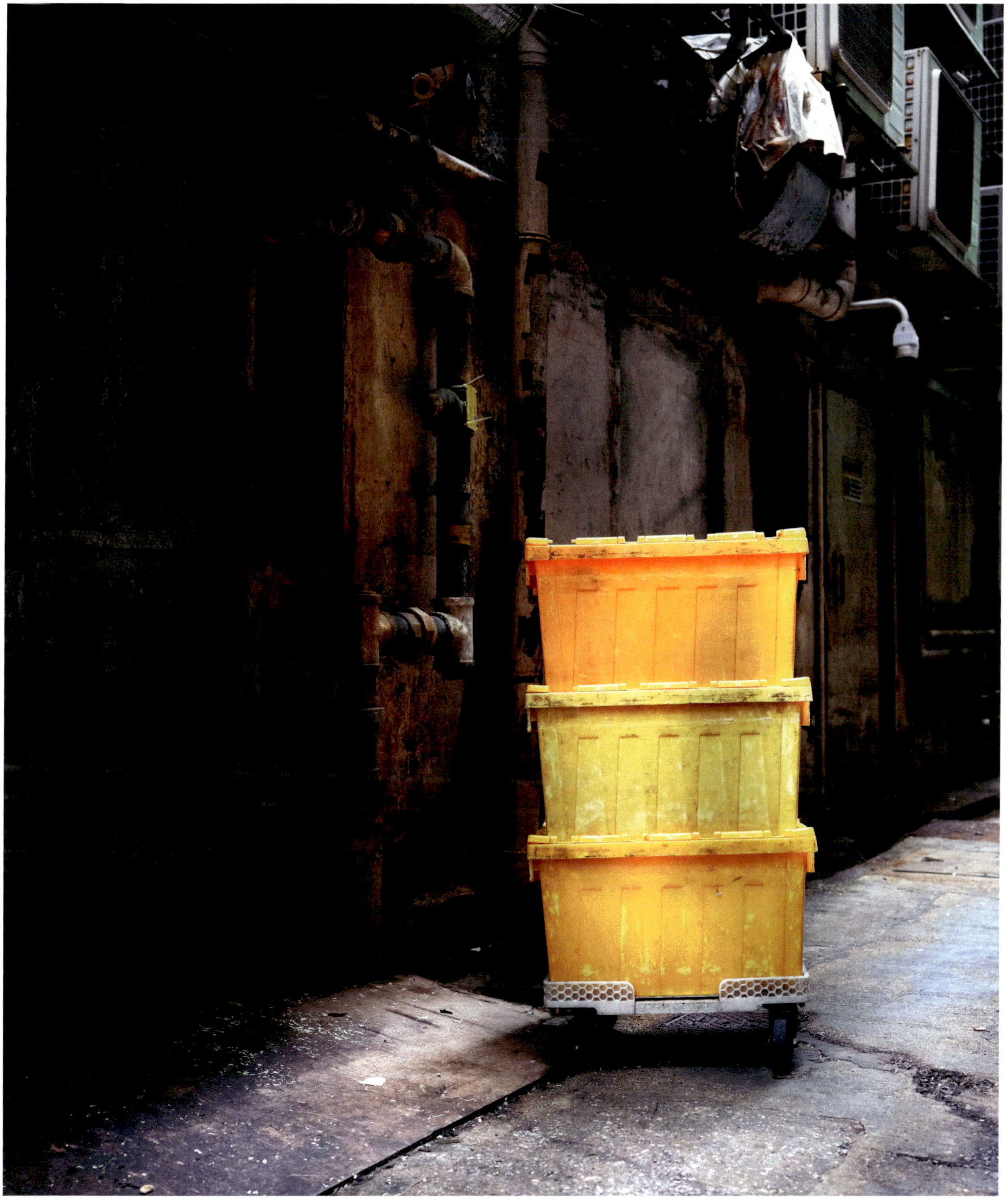

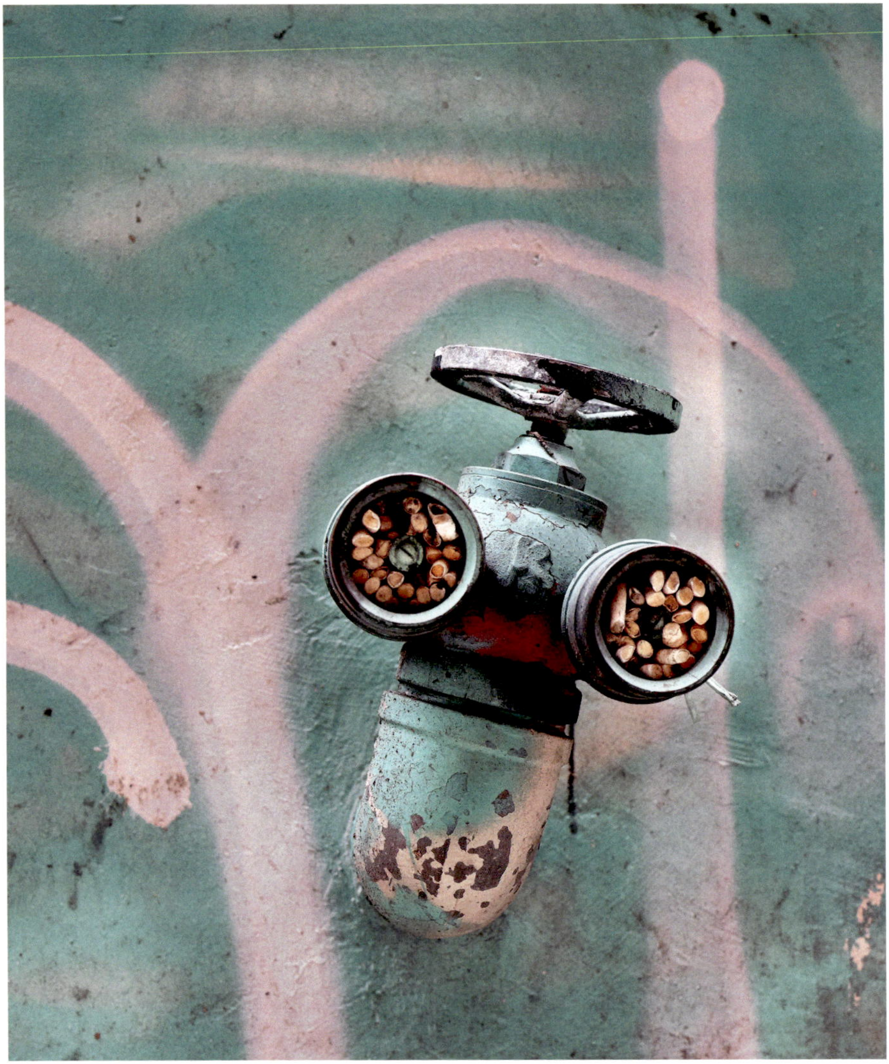

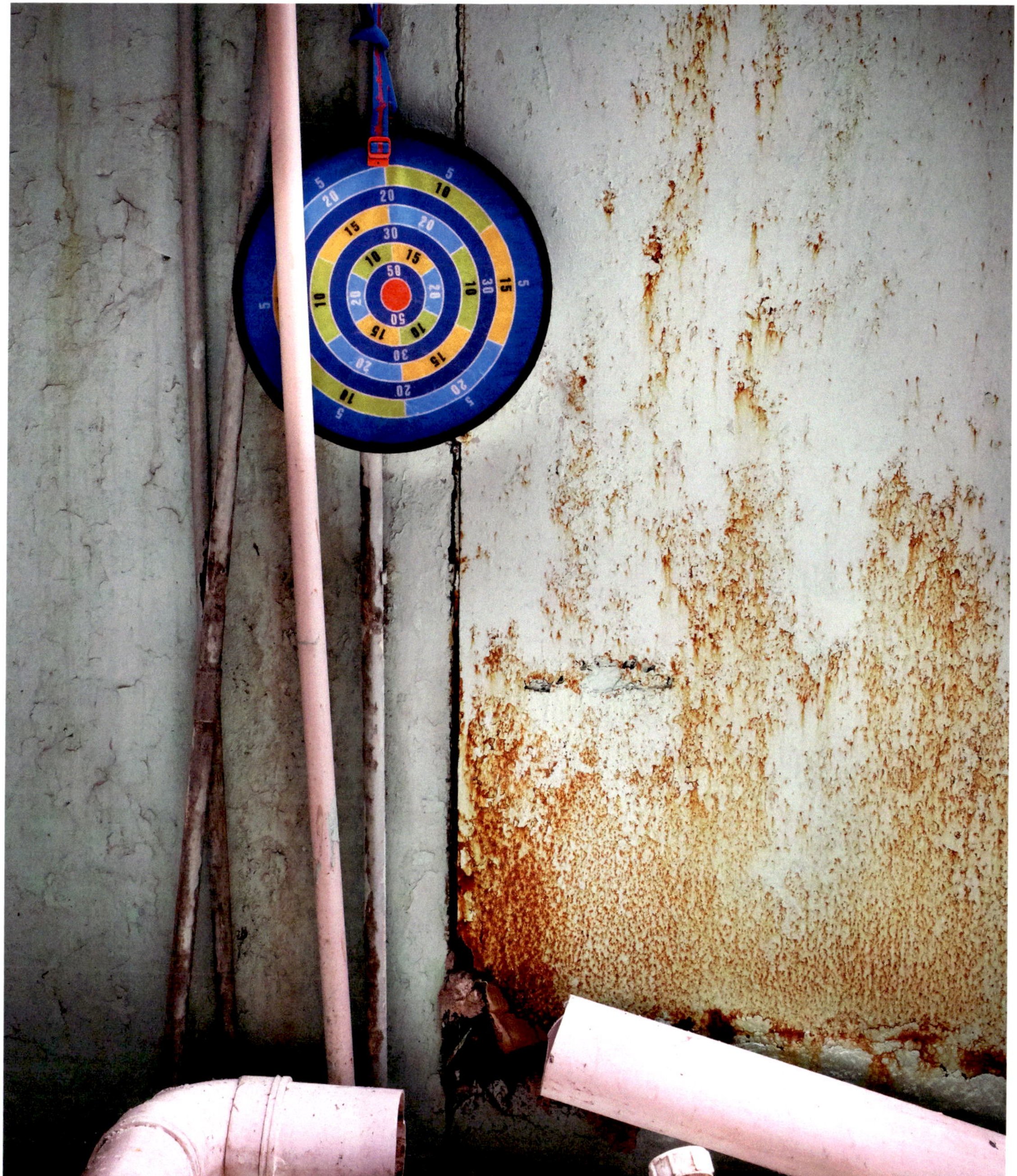

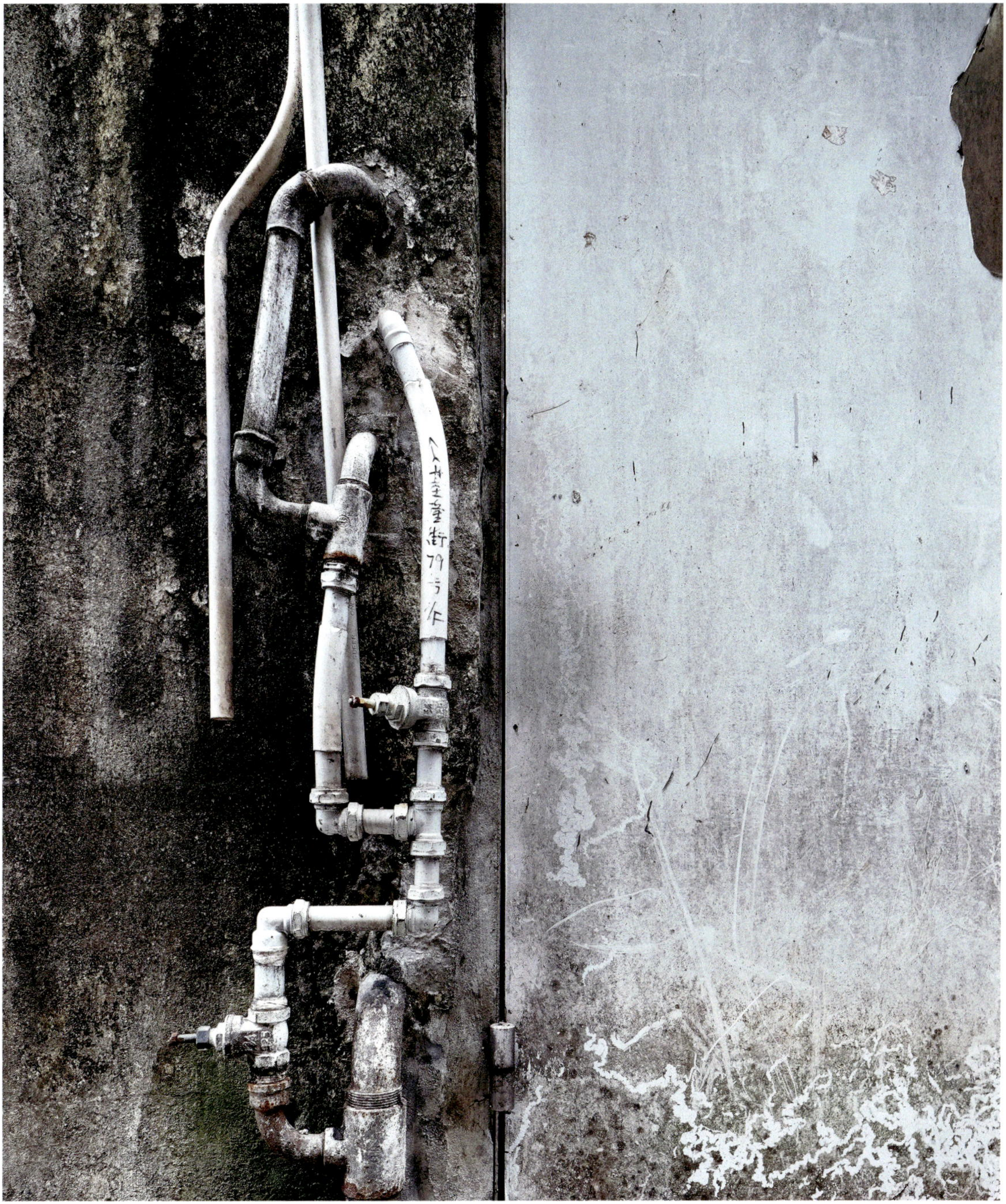

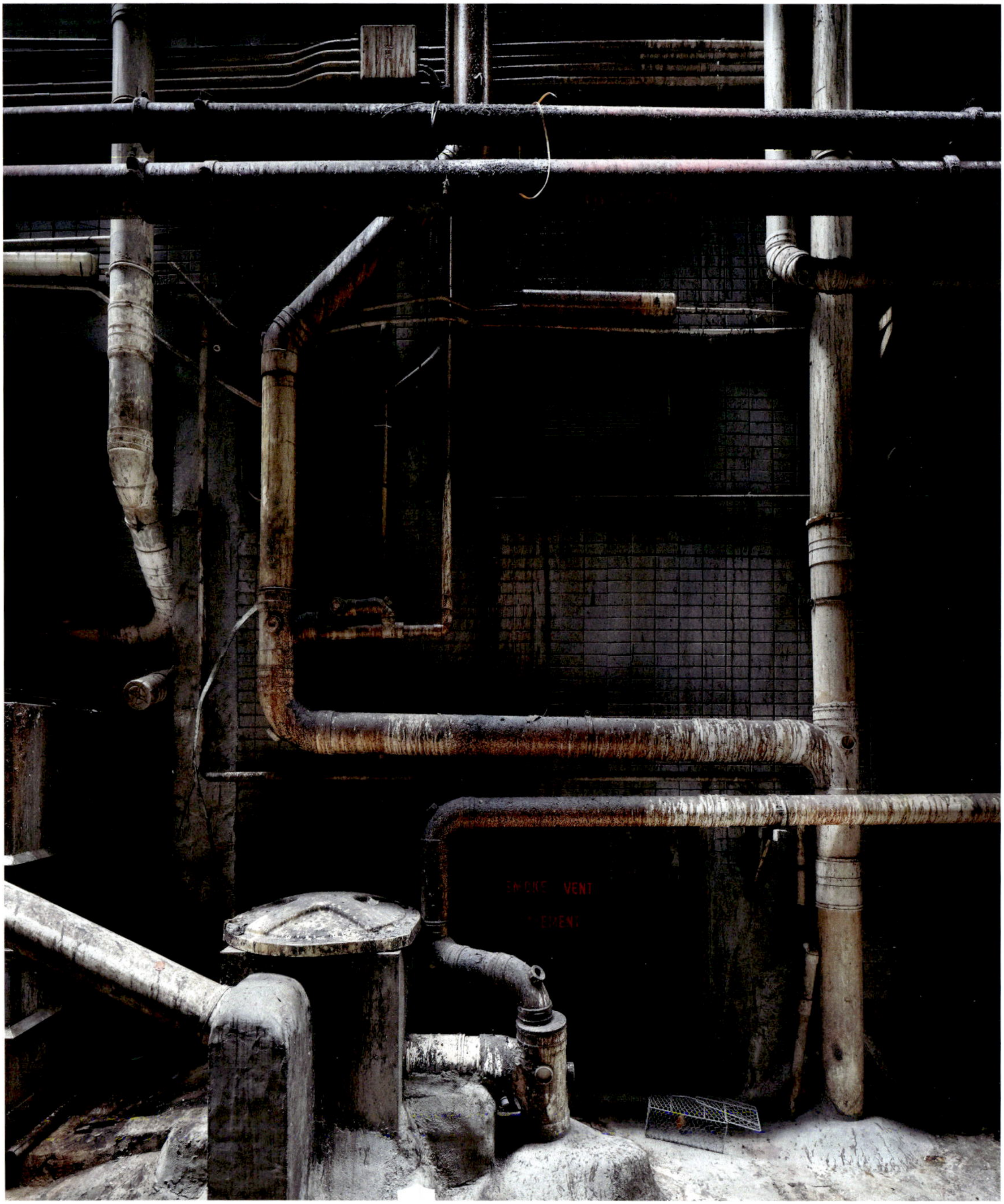
VENT

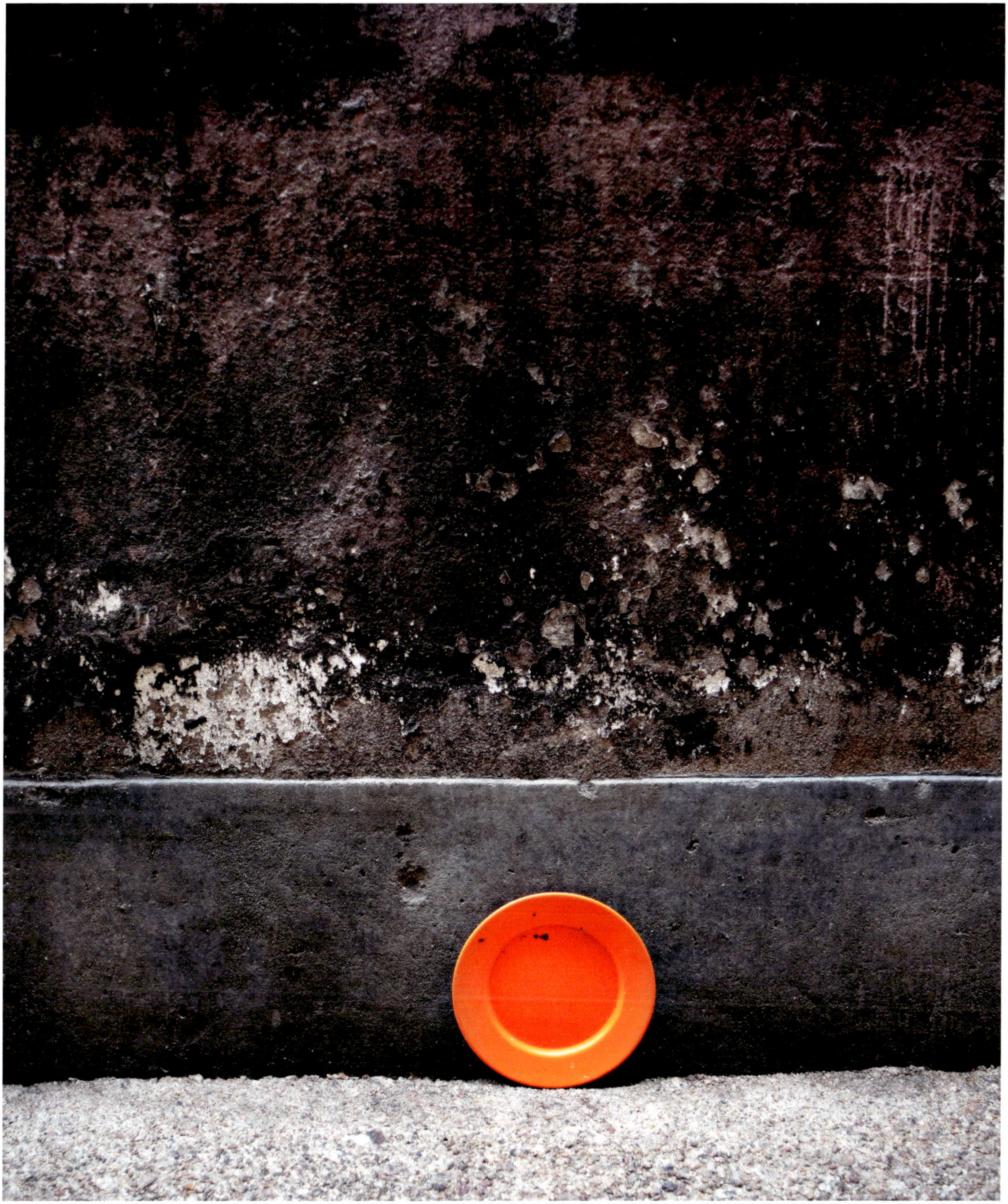

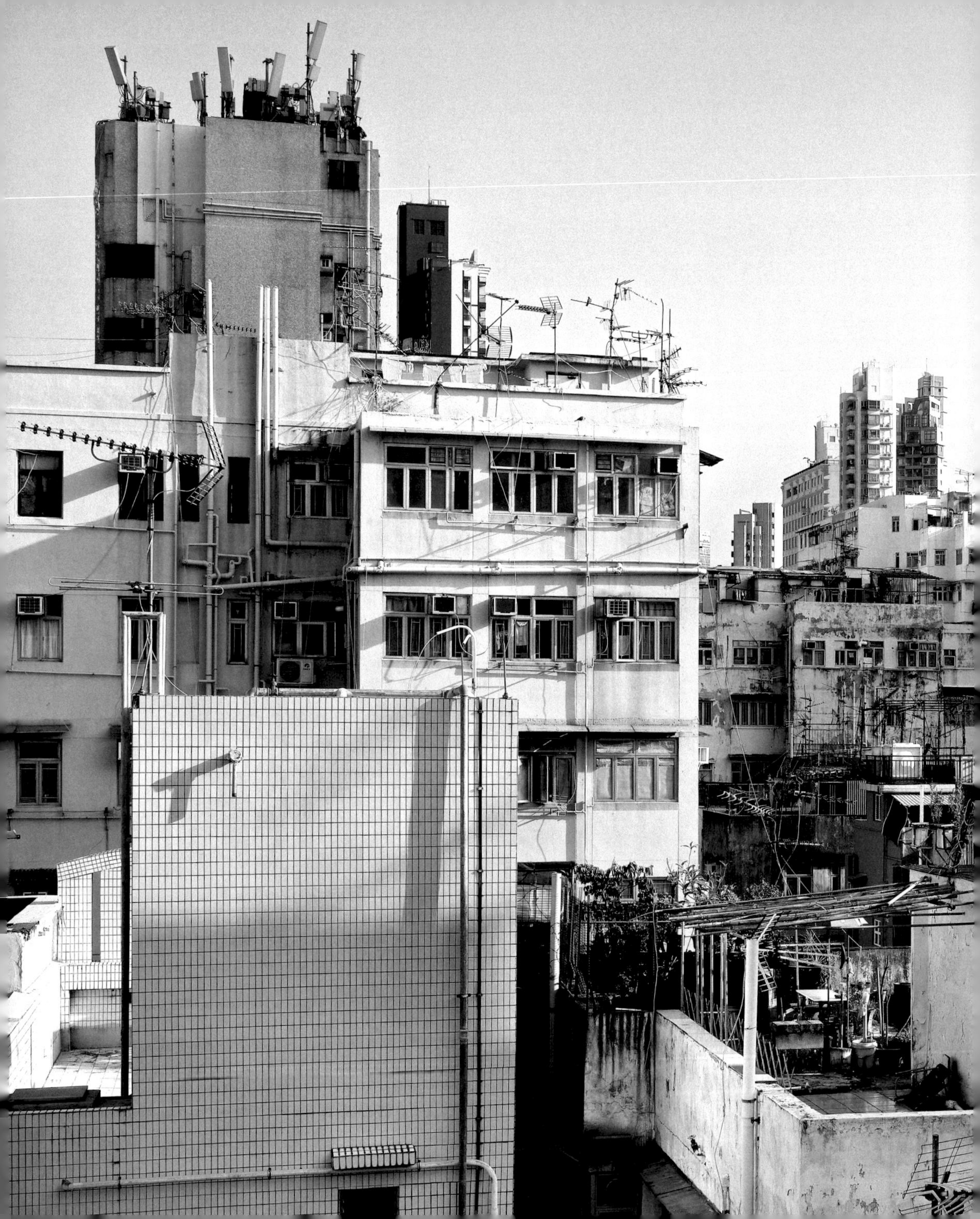

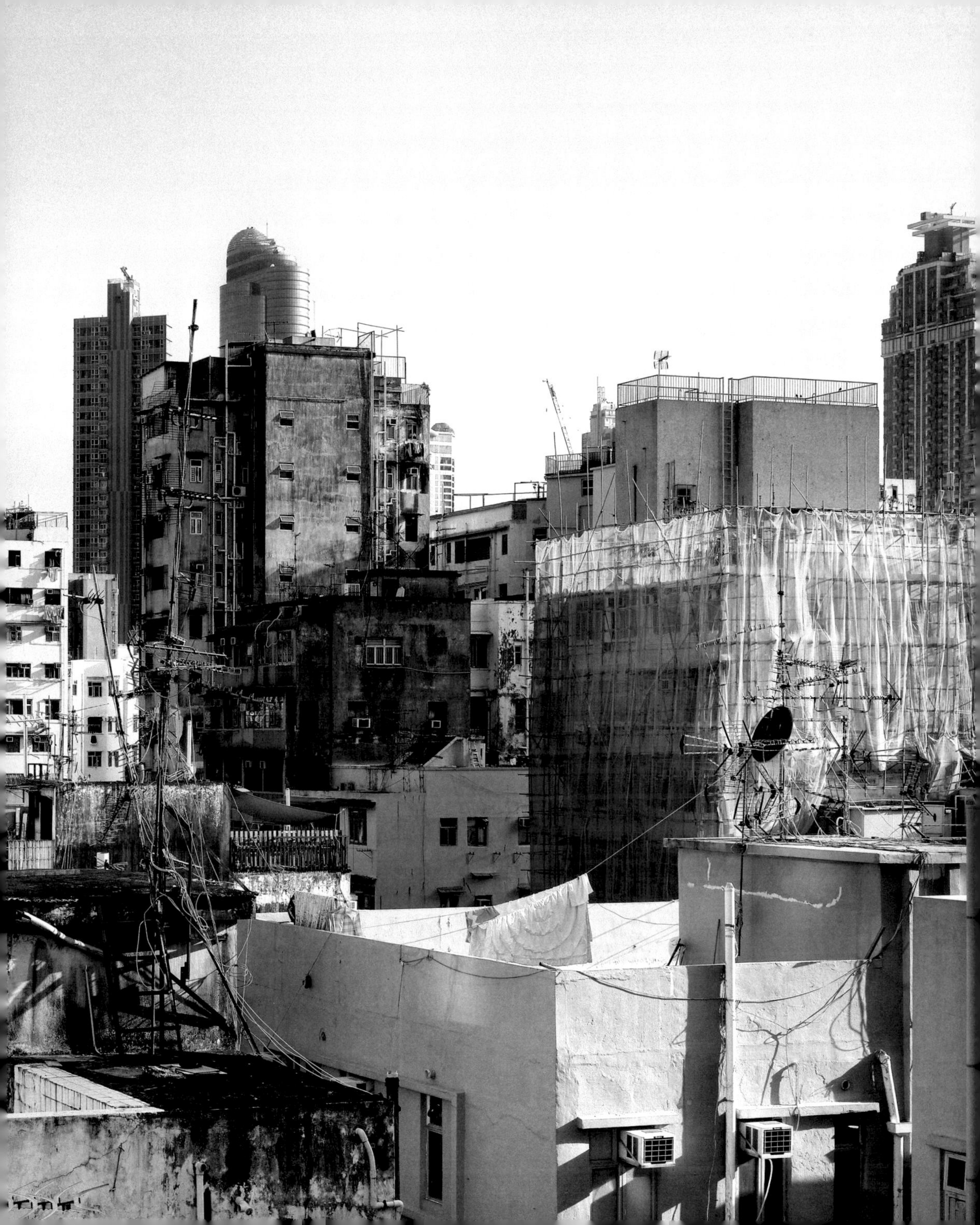

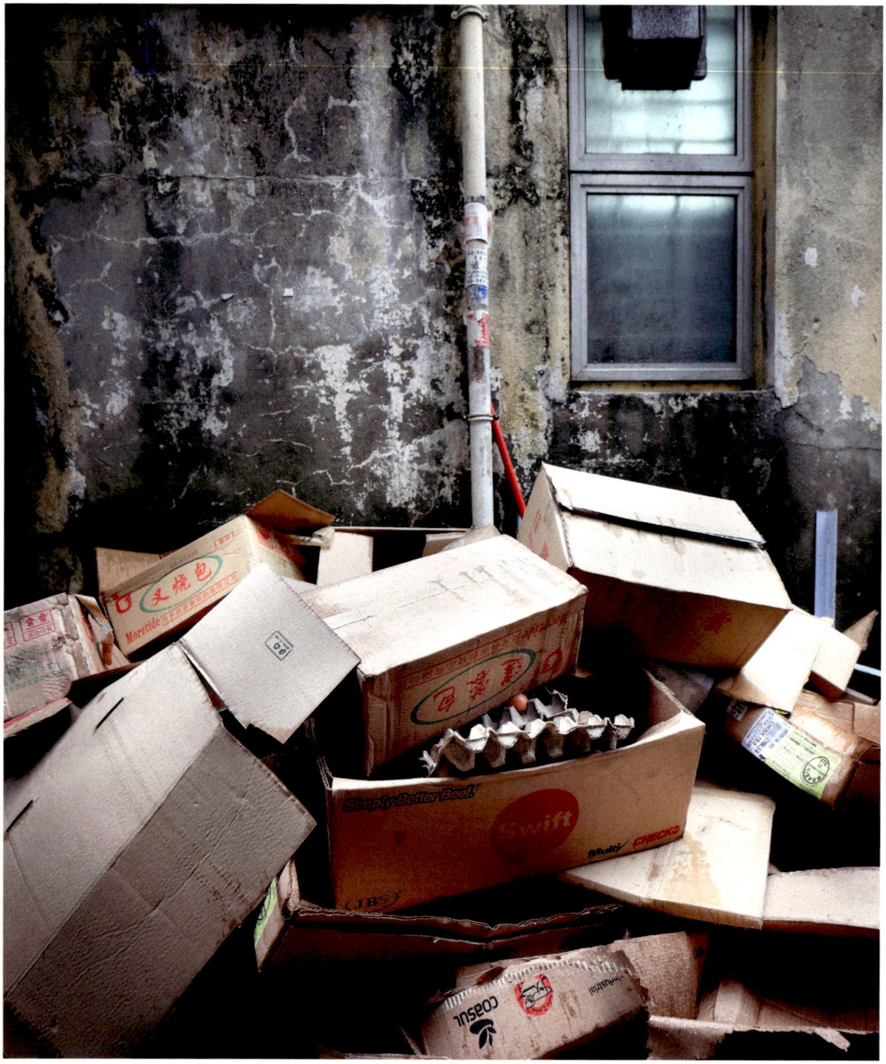
叉燒包
Moretide
Simply Better Beef.
Swift

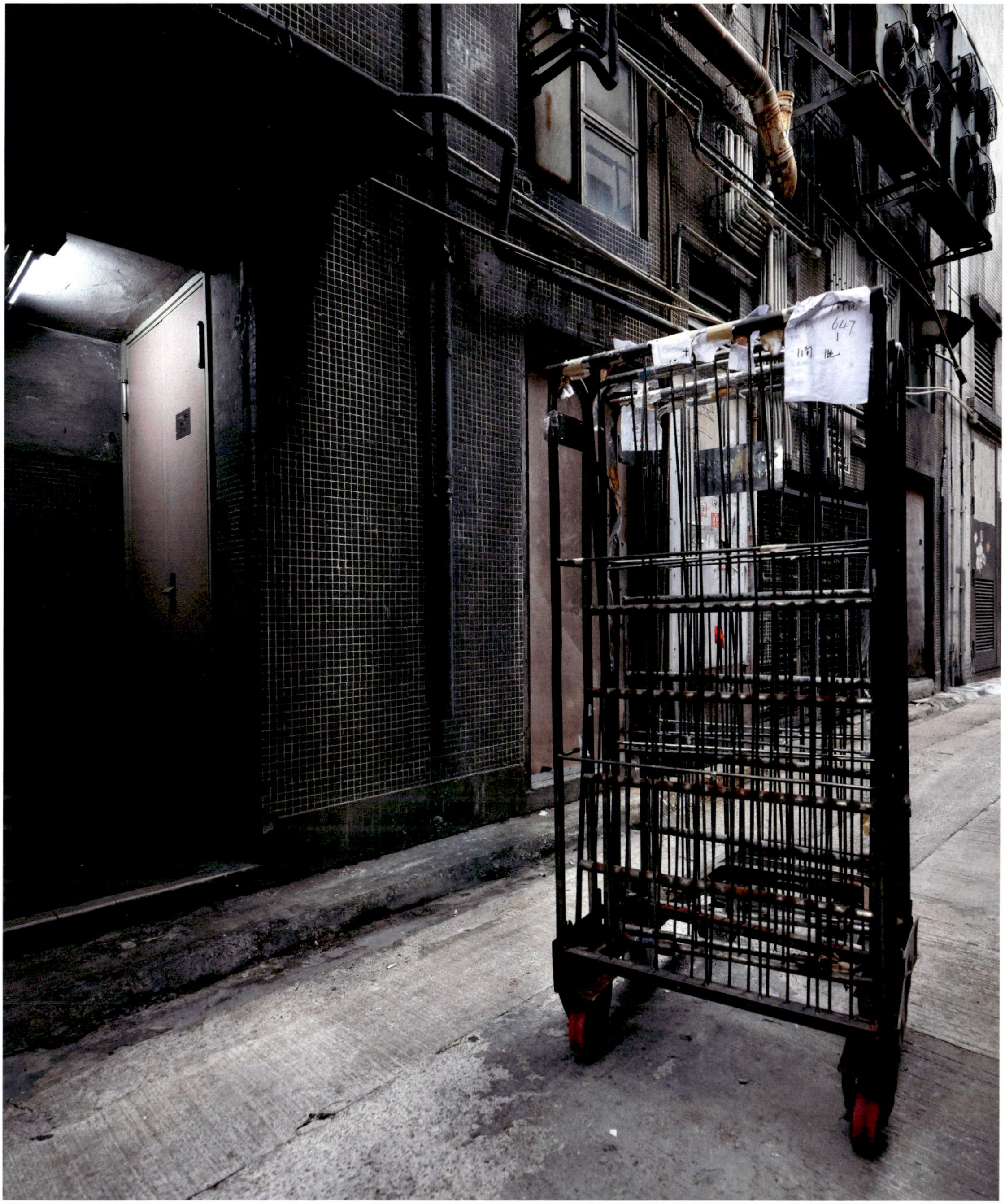

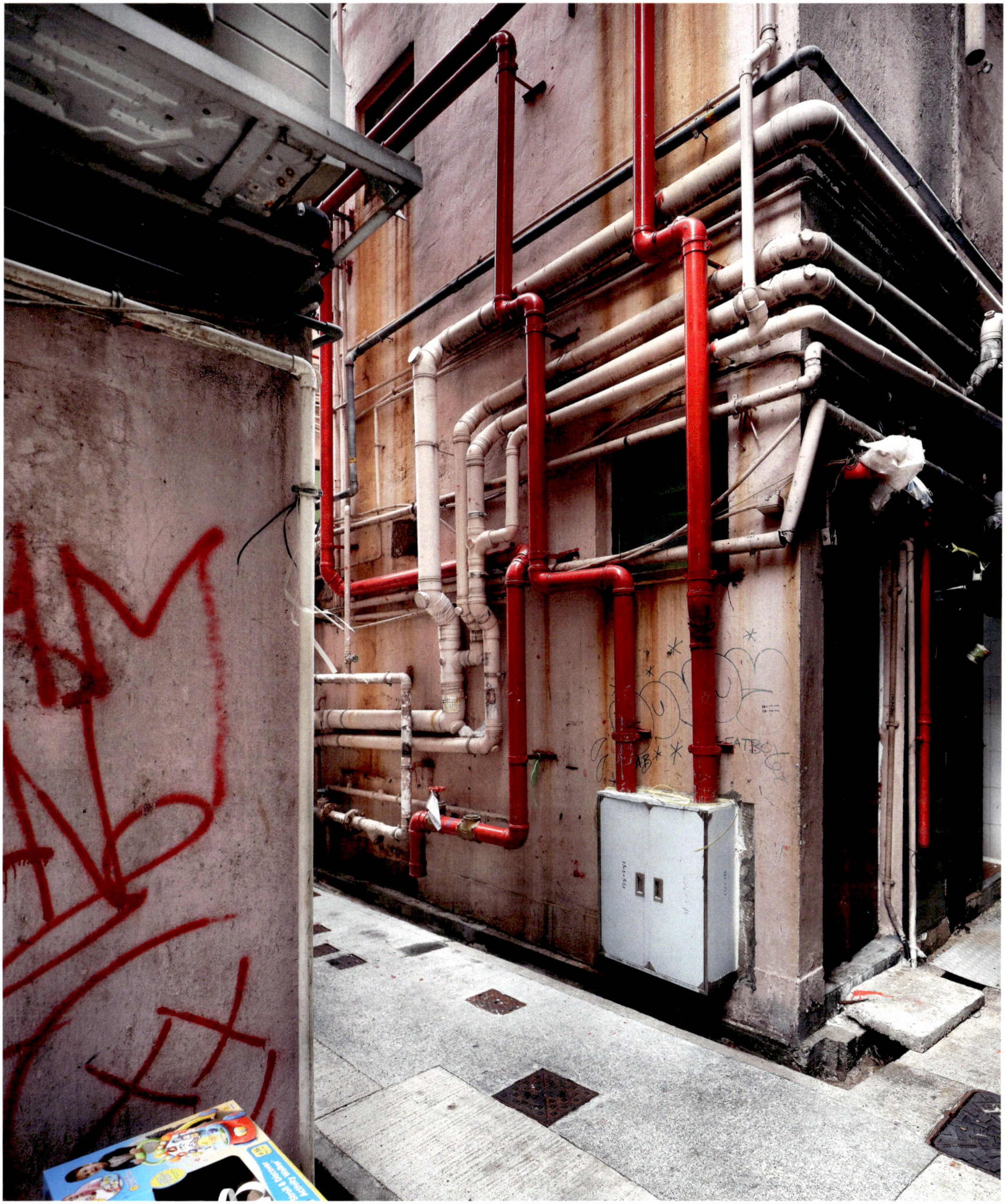

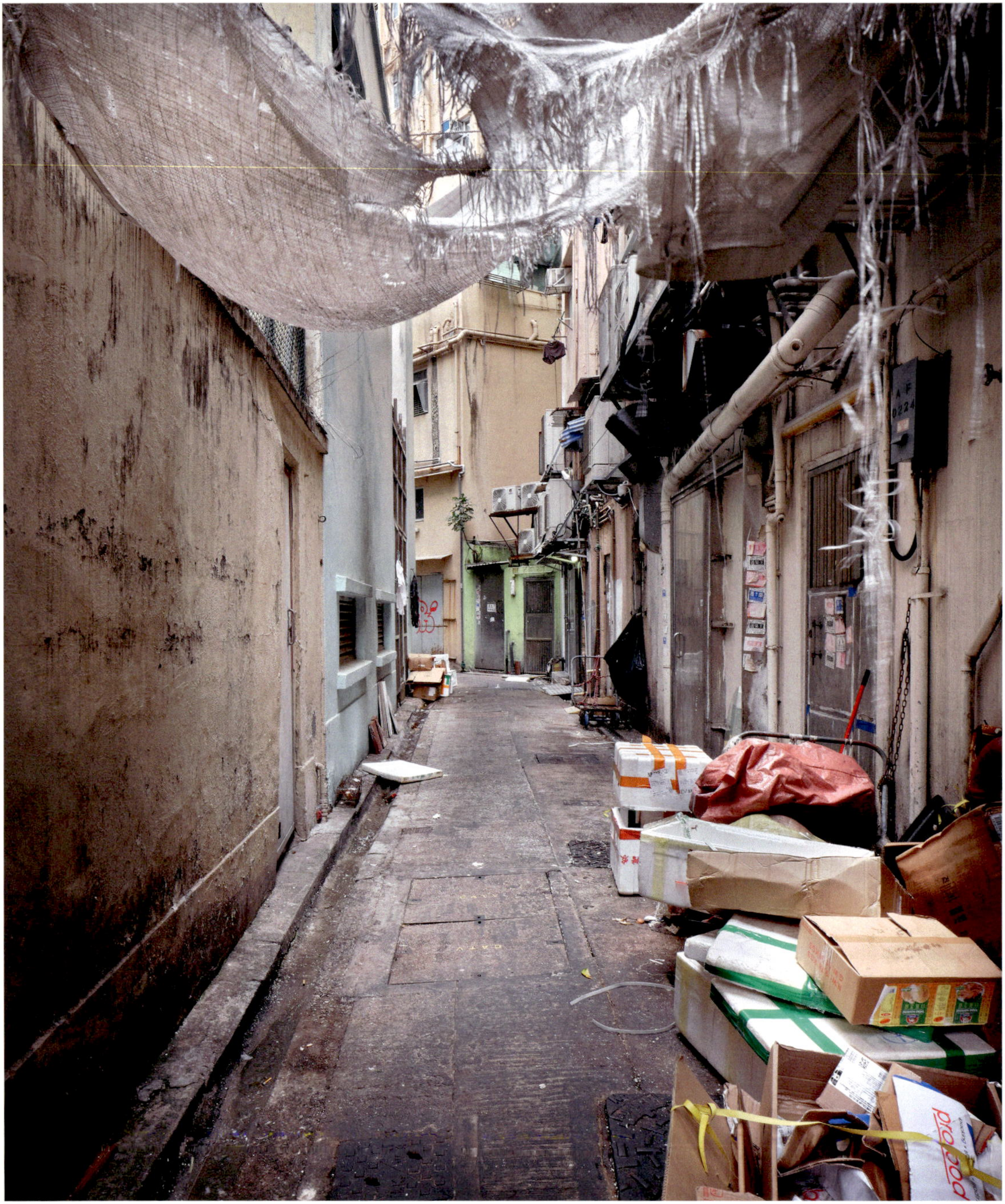

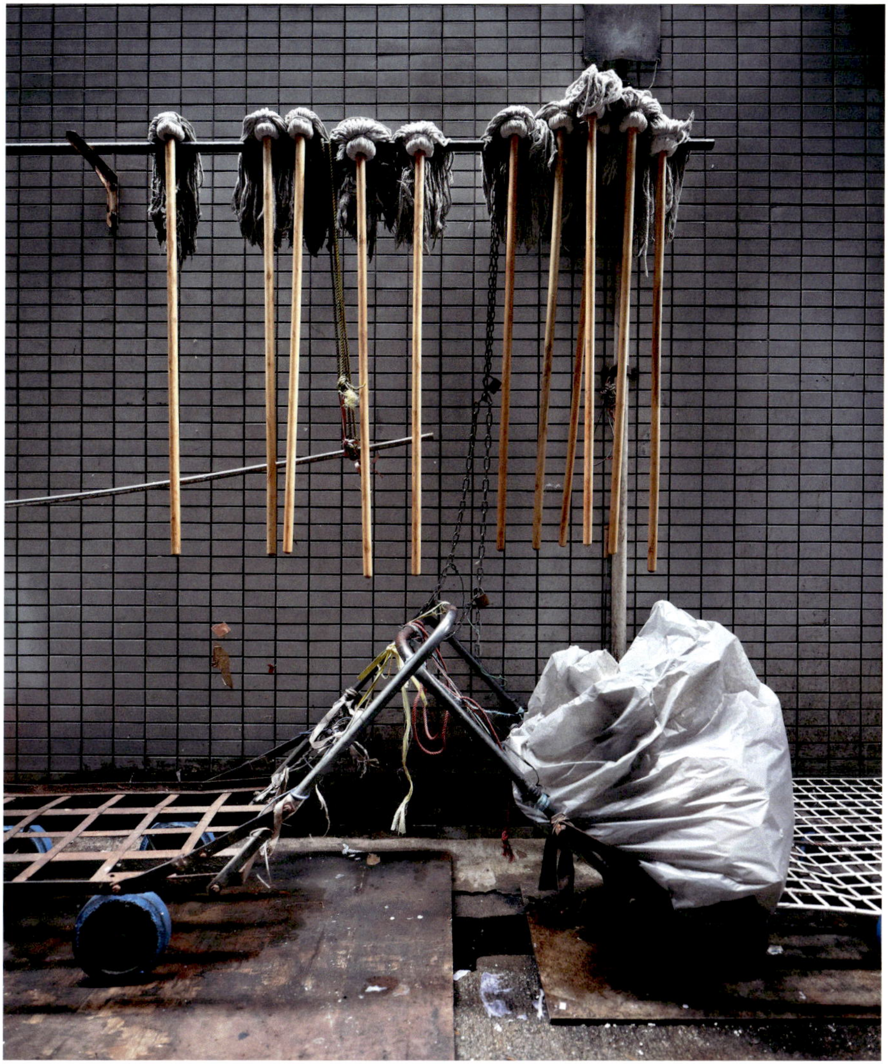

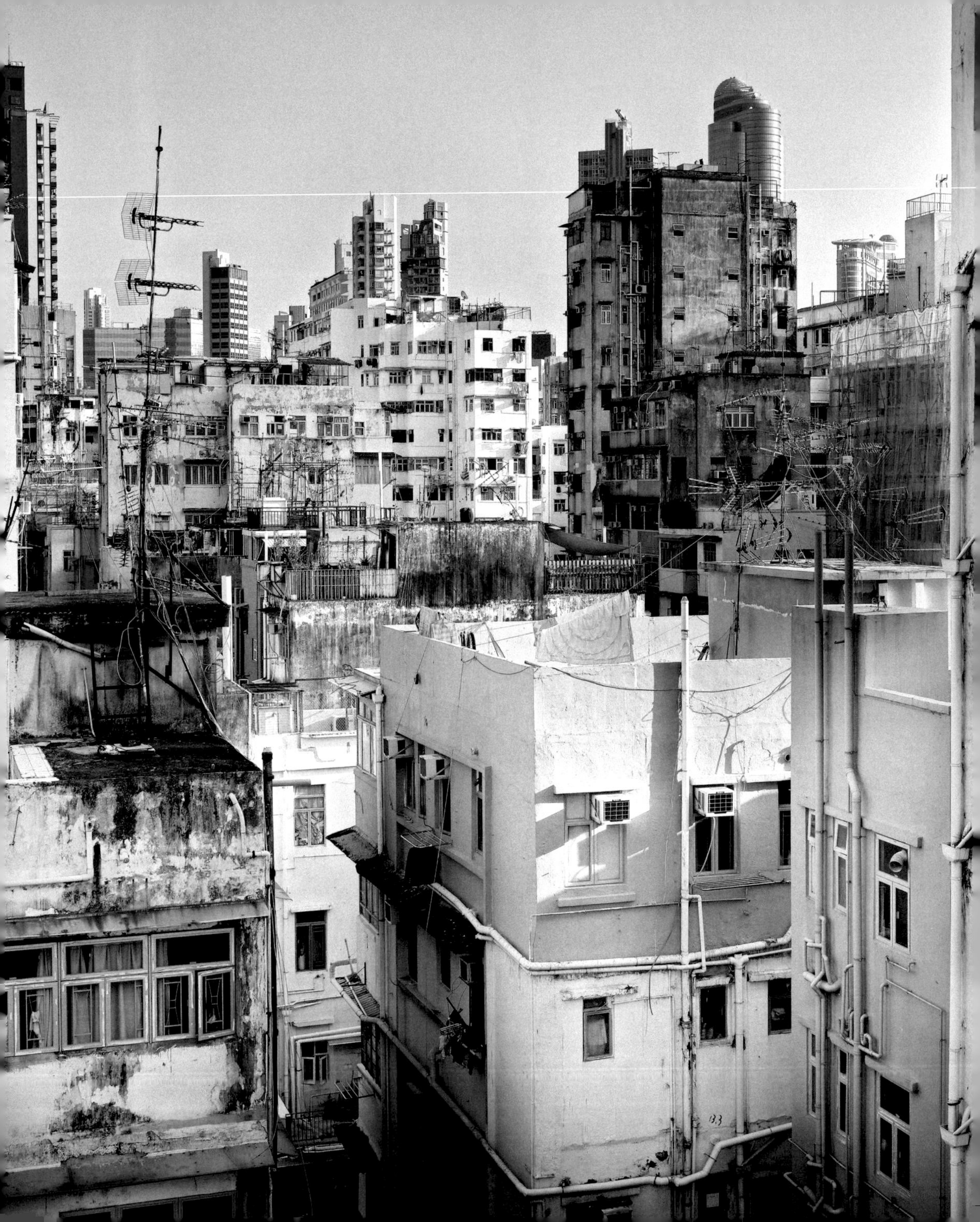

## 午 Afternoon

She speaks Thai, Mandarin, Cantonese, Hakka.

Says good morning to everyone. She wears a blue and yellow uniform, picks up trashbags around the neighbourhood, brings them to the collection point.

Three times a day is not enough. The work is payed per piece, not enough for the rent.

Newly arrived tourists and busy residents swarm the sunny streets, her garbage trolley circumnavigates them skillfully, drawing smooth trajectories, autopilot choreographies, where human and machine blend definitively: to each push corresponds a pull, highest mastery gets no praise.

This eight million metropolis produces fifteen thousand tonnes of waste daily and doesn't honour human lives. The exchange that can be named is not what's truly exchanged. The precarious are the load-bearing, supporting columns of Hong Kong's worldly development. Wisdom knows it is the ephemeral that grants the eternal.

Only in the solace of the alley's shadow her yellow gloves can finally hang loose. Eating from her lunchbox. Sleeping on the garbage trolley. Watching an episode or connecting with her family through her smartphone.

Like the mind explorers of the ancient *via negativa* method, Matthias' photographs articulate the distance between an imperceptible glimpse of afternoon and its permanent shared memory, the process of an image becoming a psycho-geography of time.

The alley is our secret passage and silent backbone boulevard, the daily oasis of memories she will gather tomorrow, to make sense of today.

These photographs gather the whispers of the local unsung multitude, channel them into a powerful chorus of urban legacy. They reveal a deeper, fundamental human necessity rather than empty, petty respectabilities. The arrogance of individuals claiming their conscious space in the narration dissolves to unleash the highest potential of the most sensitive, heterogeneous commonalty.

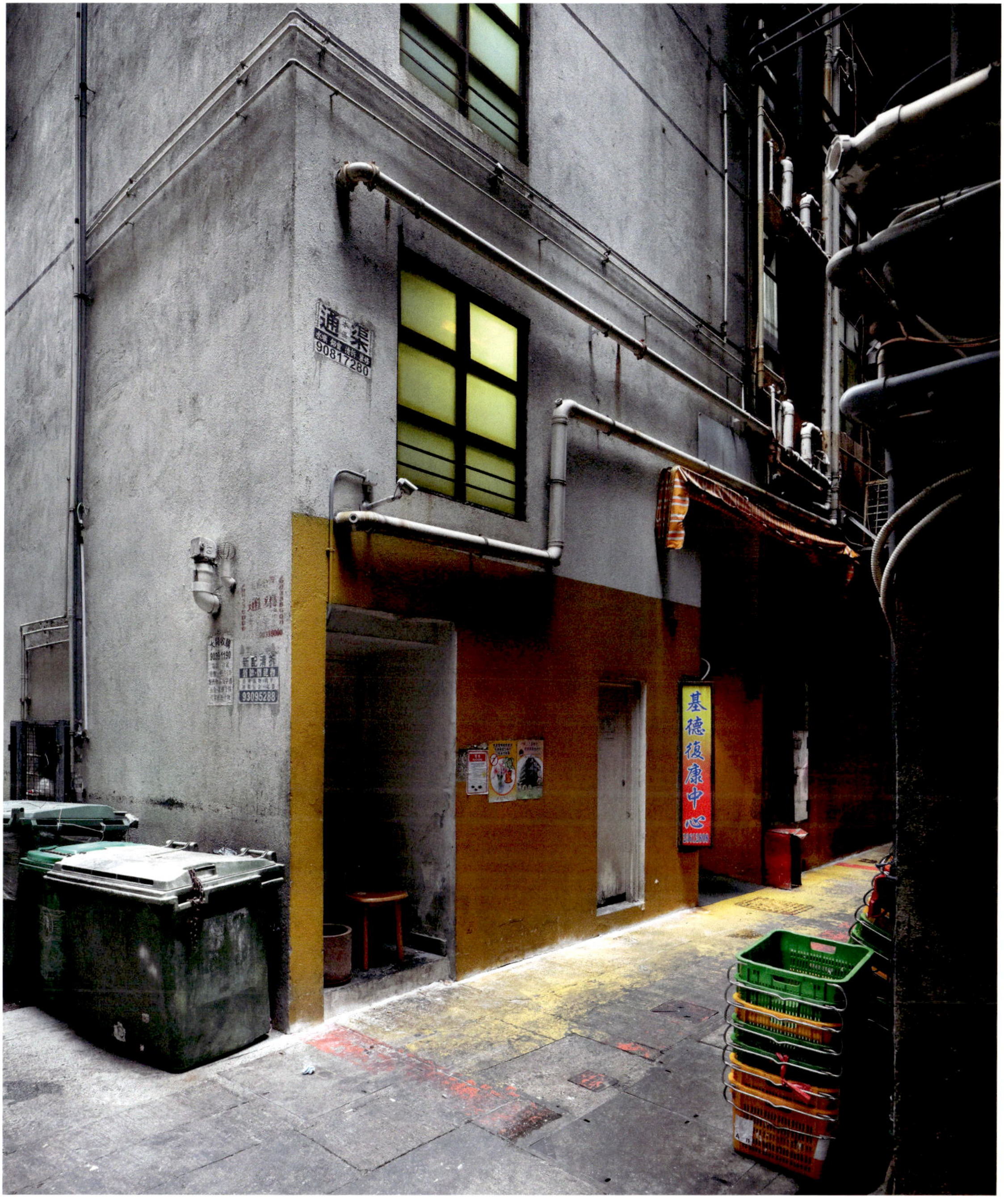
通渠
90817280
93095288
基德復康中心

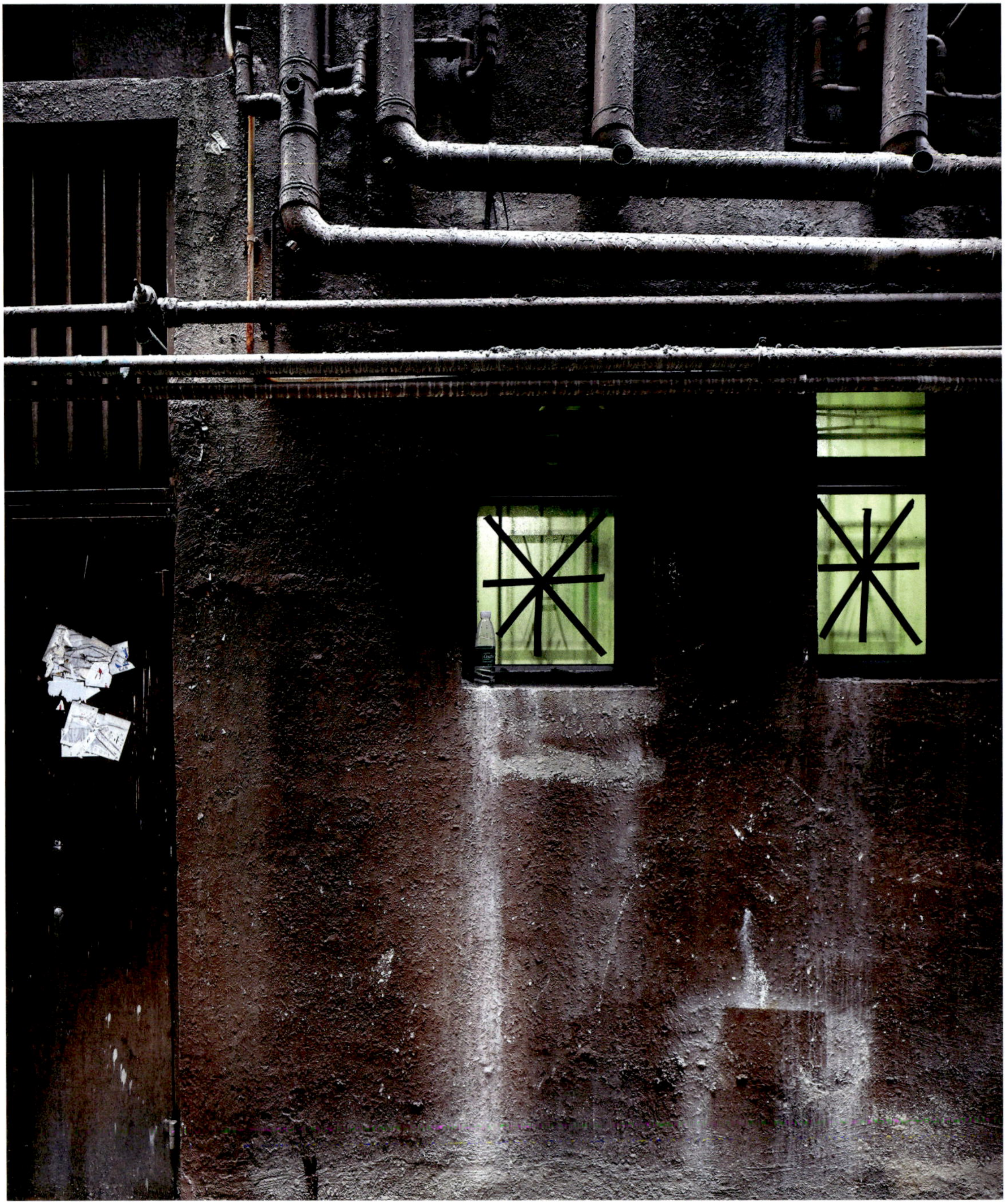

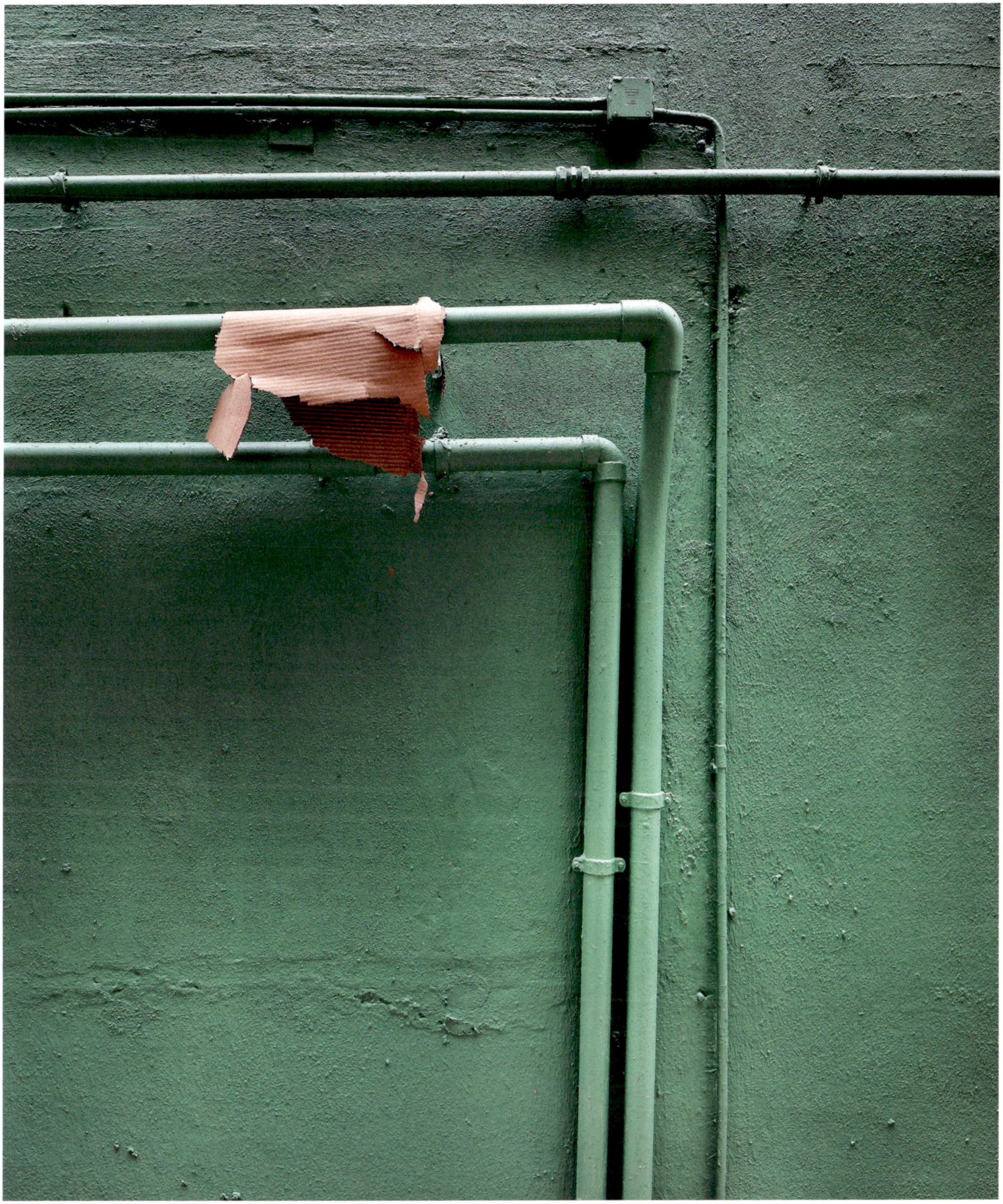

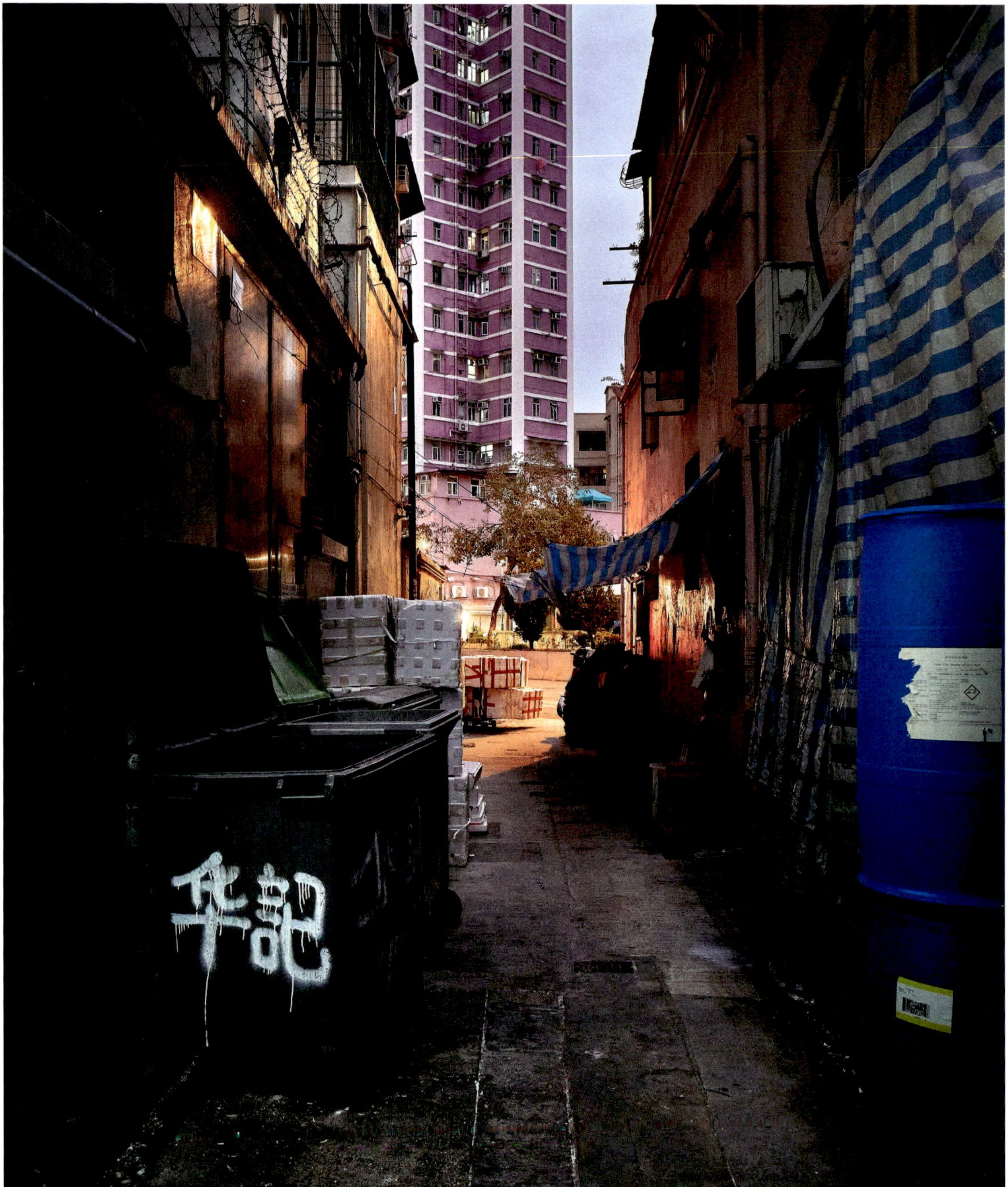

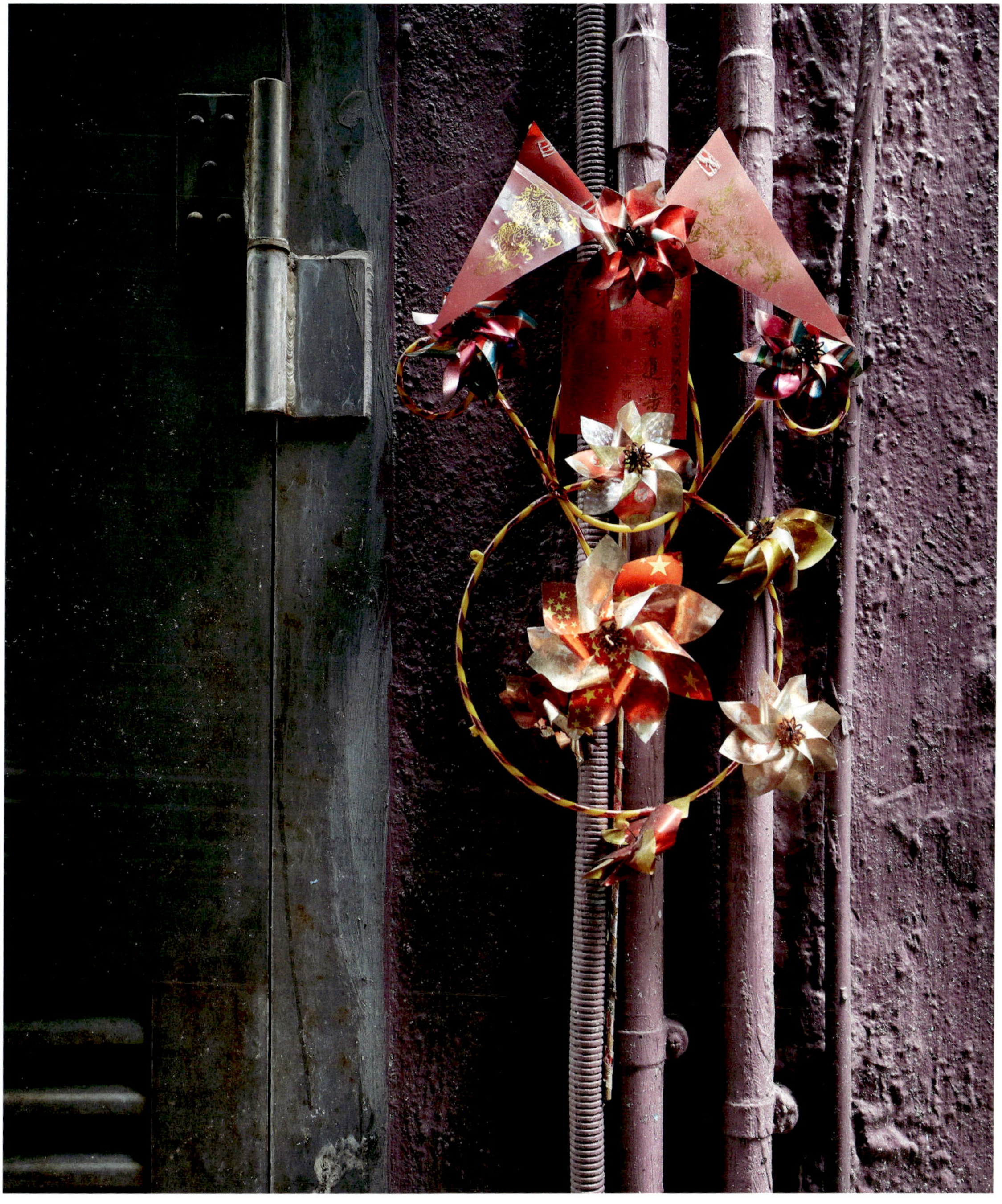

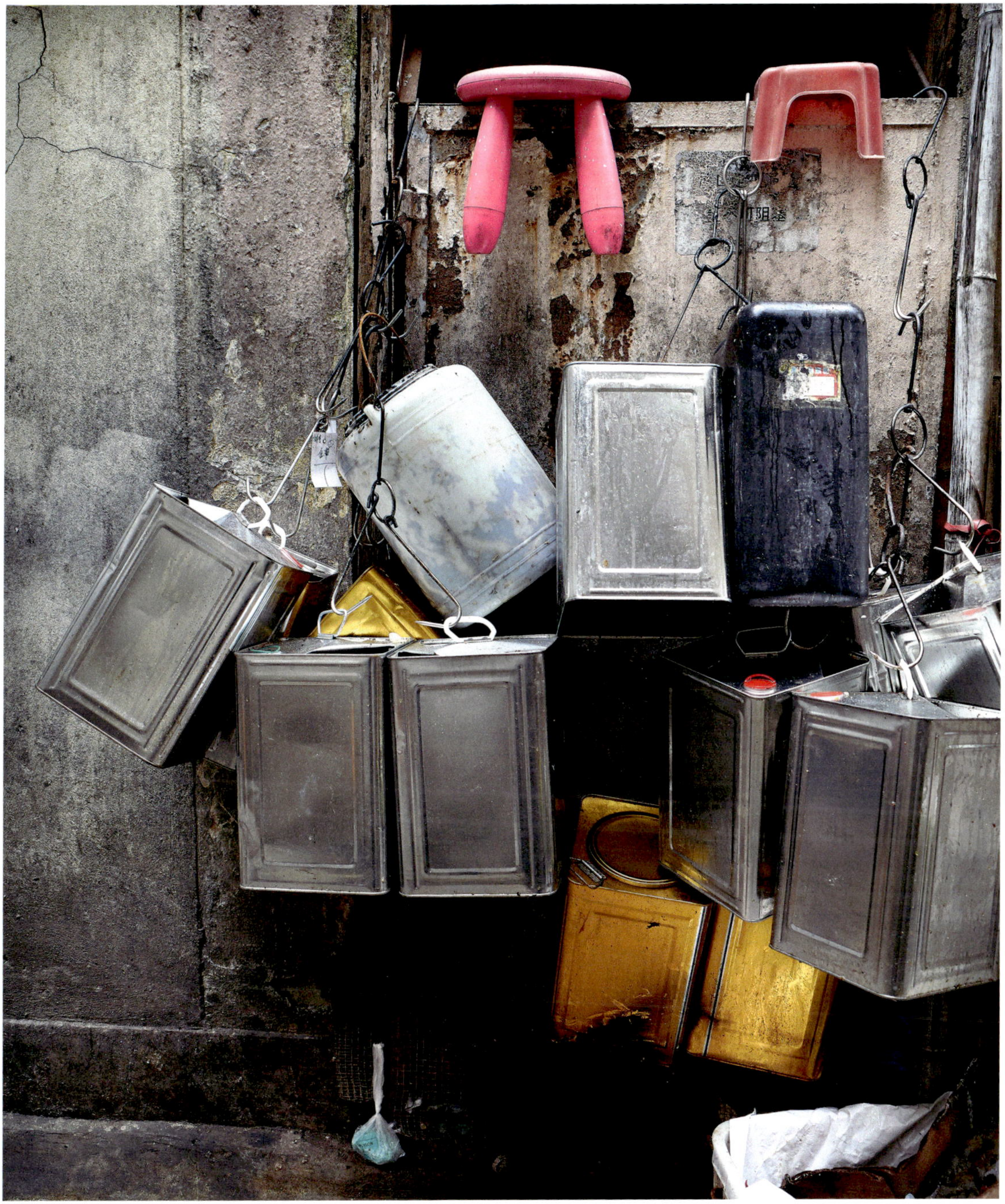

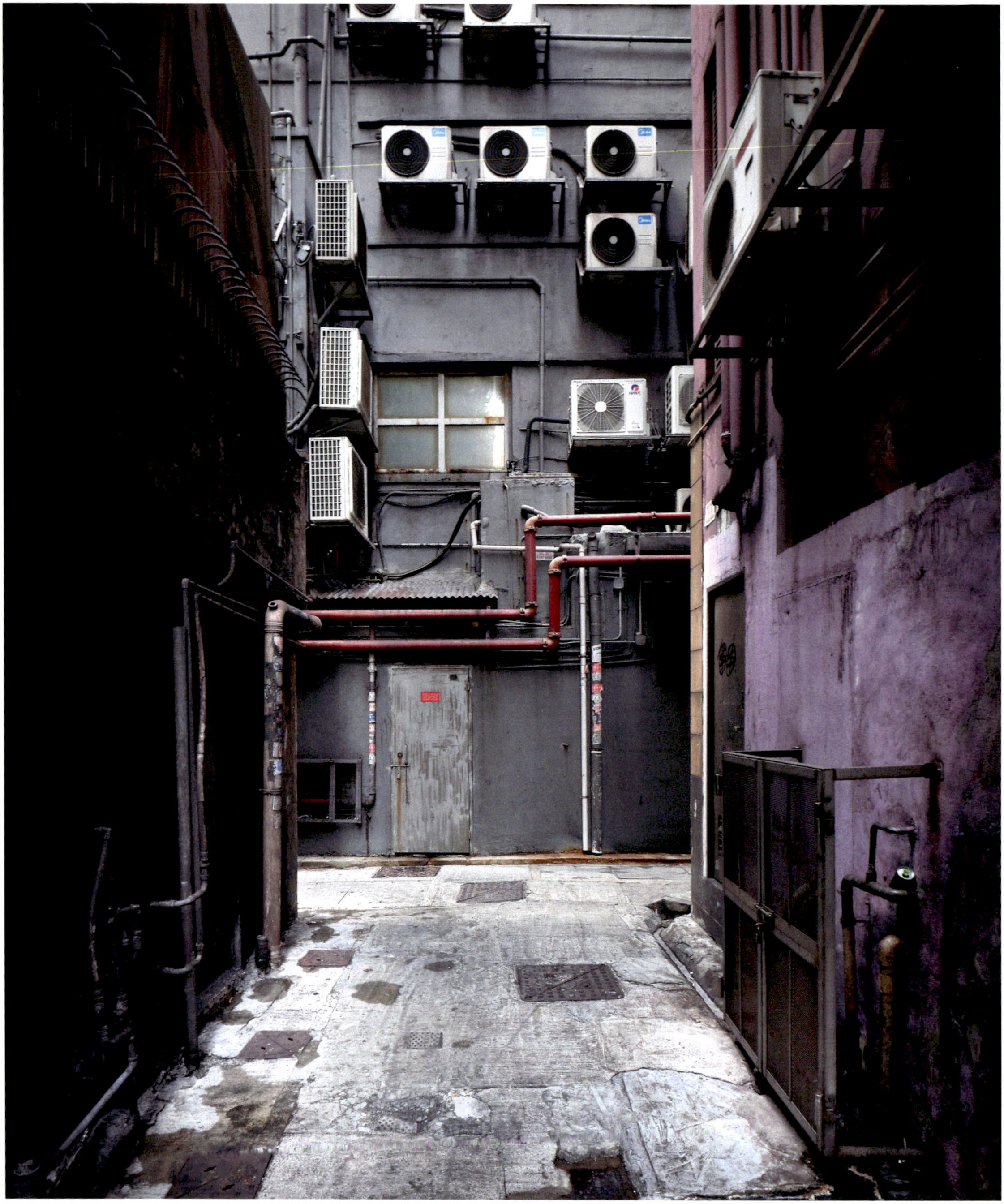

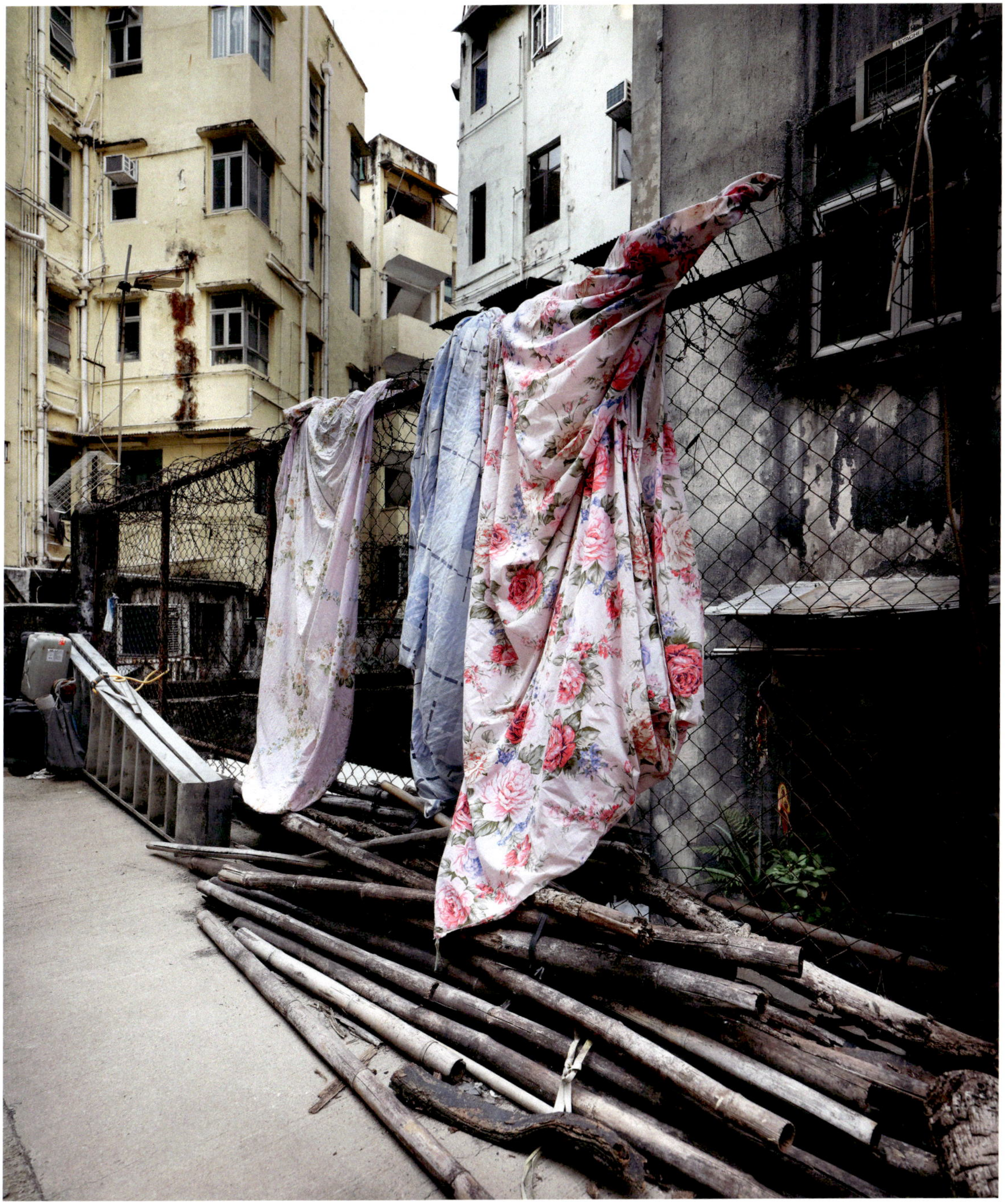

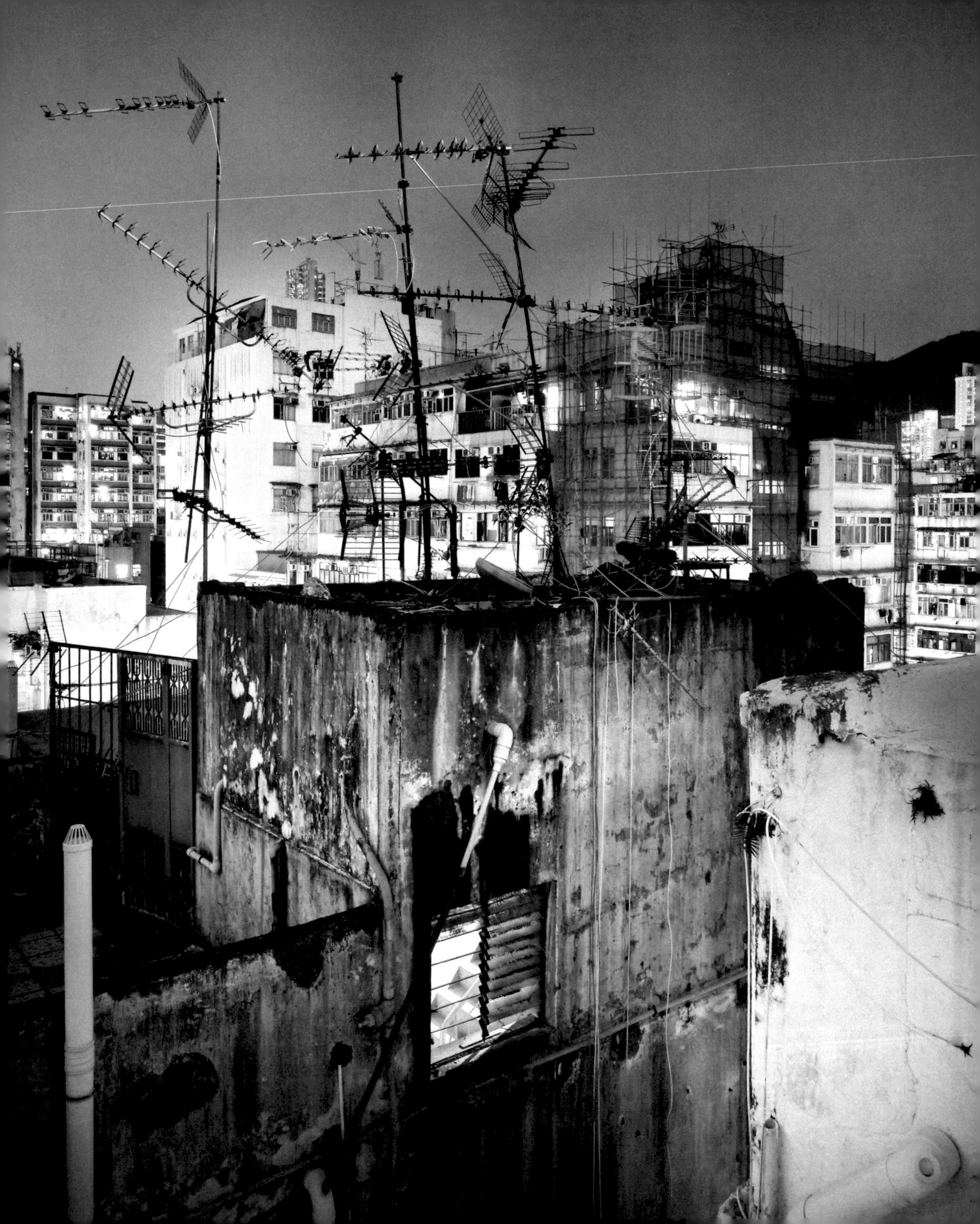

## 晚 Night

Embraced by steep, unevenly lit concrete walls on all sides, the alley does not sip moonlight.

At night, strangers uncomfortably share humidity in the dark. Some look around furtively while coming home, some grab their late privacy for a fleeting tenderness.

Mr Chan's headlamp nervously sorts the cartons he has piled up today, soaking them in water overnight, so Mohammad's scale will weigh them triple when they are all dried up tomorrow.

With time, memories solidify into archetypical traces of the passage of our loved ones. Deep in our subconscious rests the pre-rational manifestation of our existence.

The most powerful photographs do not display motifs superficially, they summon them from within ourselves. Matthias captures the timeless by capturing our time, subtracting what we are not, resulting in an image of who we truly are.

The feeble flickering of gaunt lightbulbs seldom scratches the deaf darkness, shining through this multi-species, multi-material anthropocene of sleepwalking.

For fifteen million years roaches have been hunted by bats, cities fail to chase them away, in its dark cracks they thrive, our presence only momentarily disturbing their feast.

Matthias' timeless instants of aesthetic purity humble and ignite the slick, soulless landscapes of urban banality, his minimalist approach pulling the veil off of urban dwelling.

Alchemical transformation weds Daoist wisdom in the early-hour mandalas of Sham Shui Po's back alleys: we are gone before the street cleaning truck wipes our traces away in the morning.

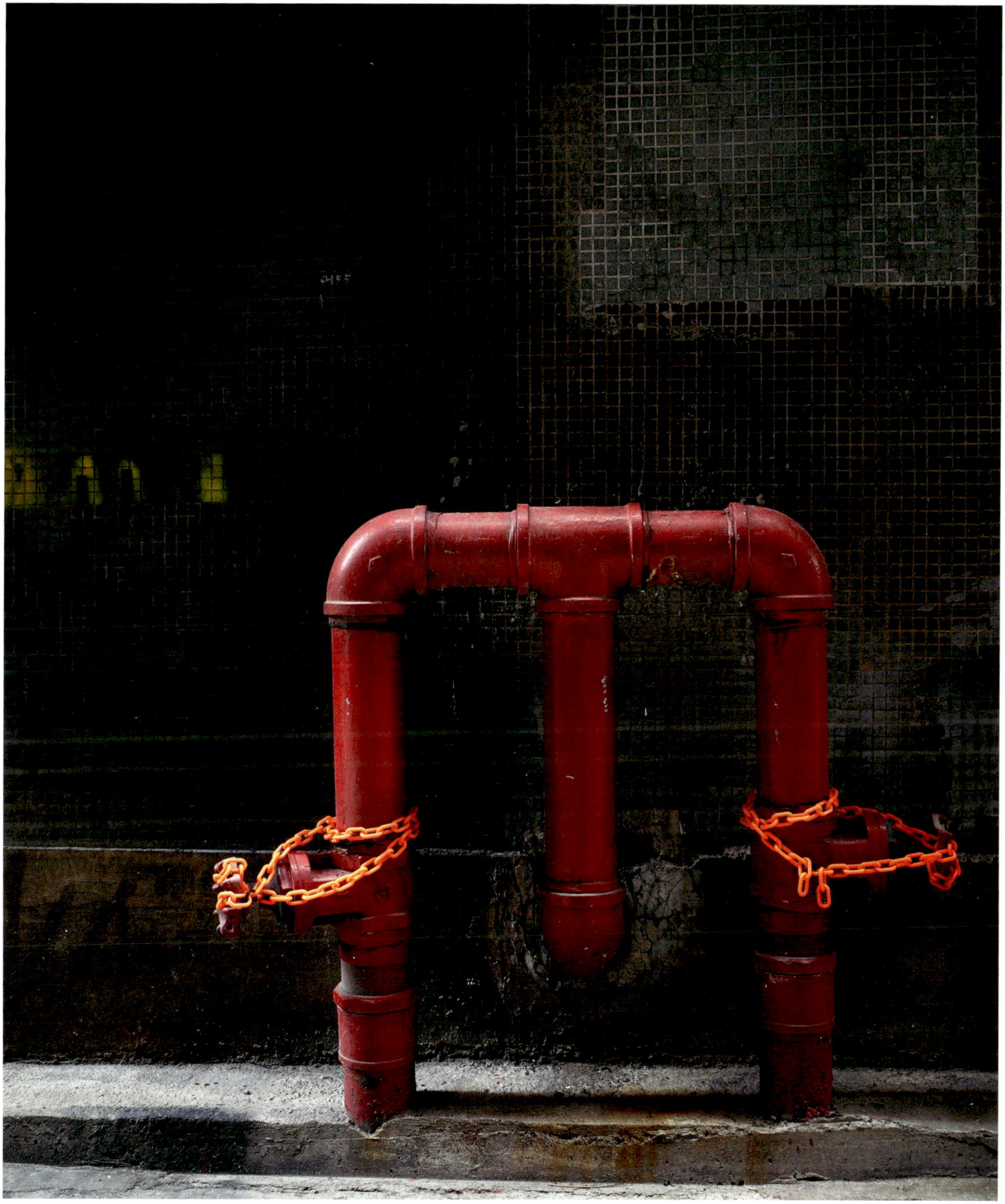

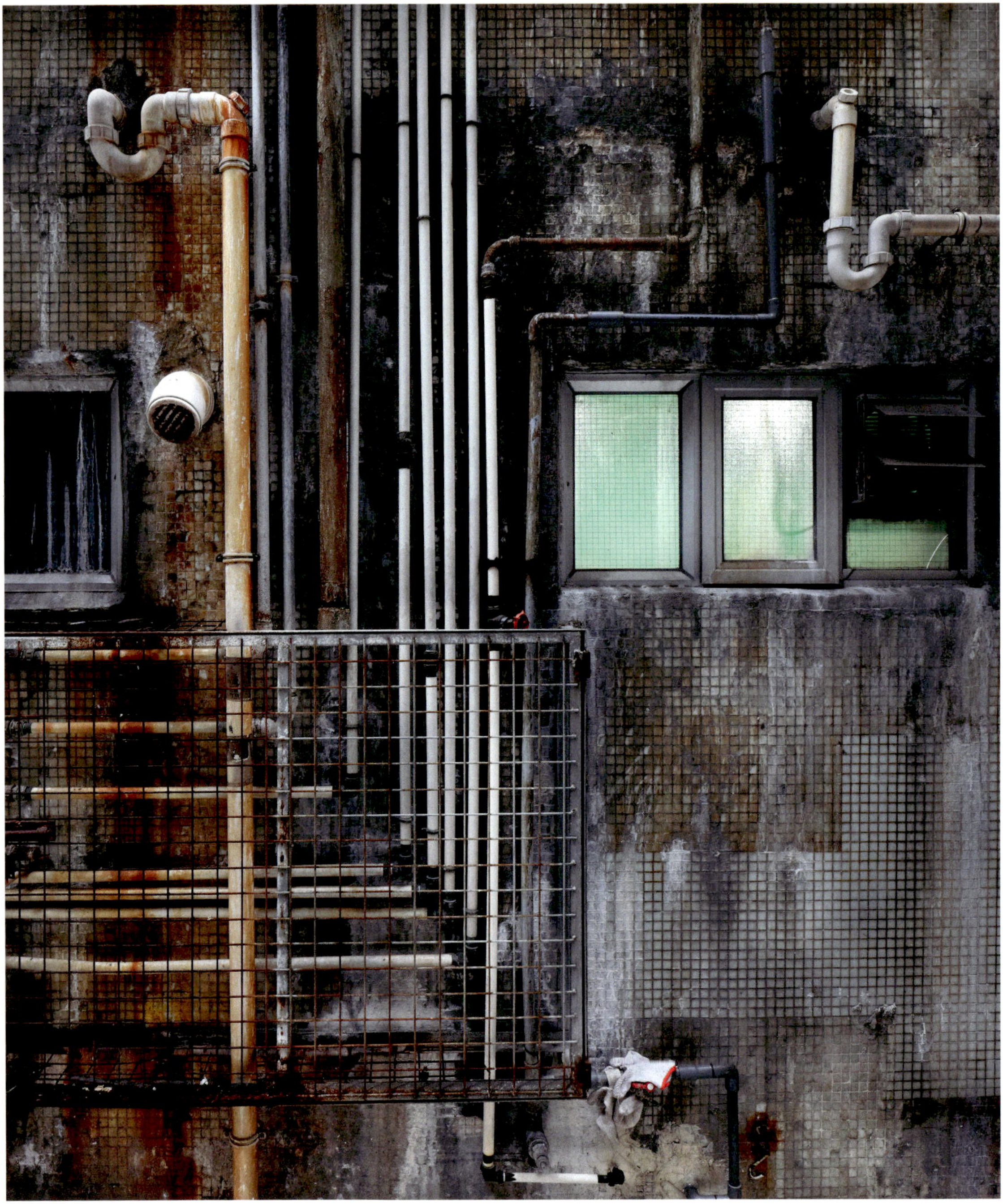

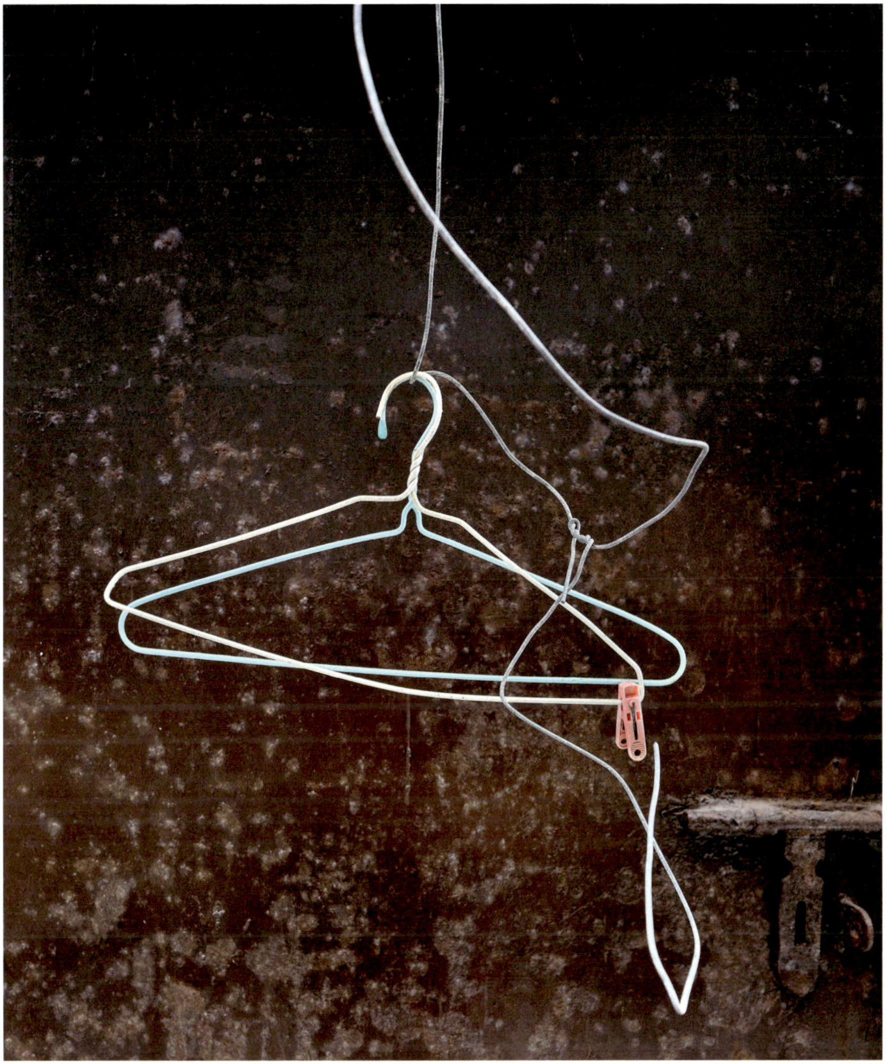

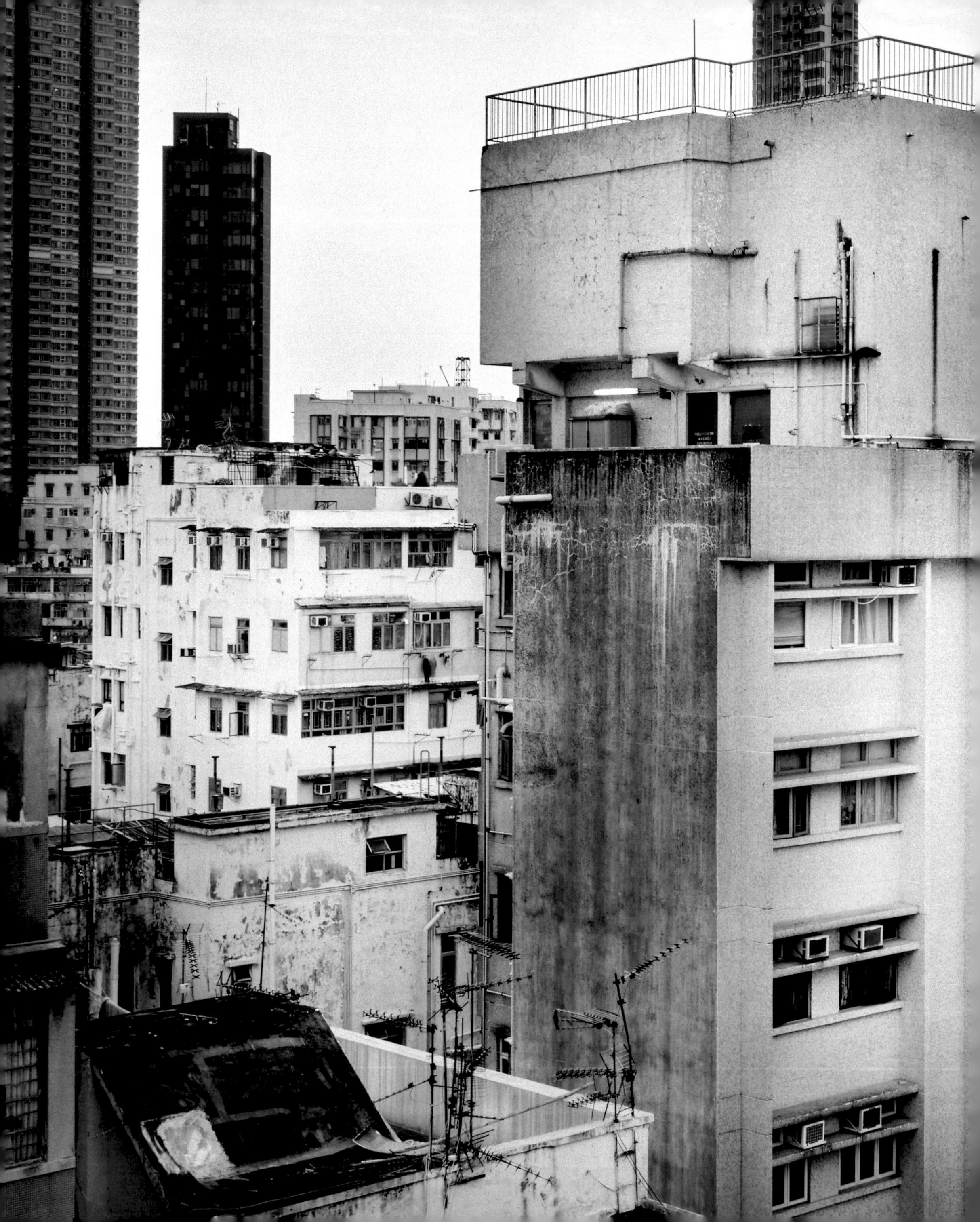

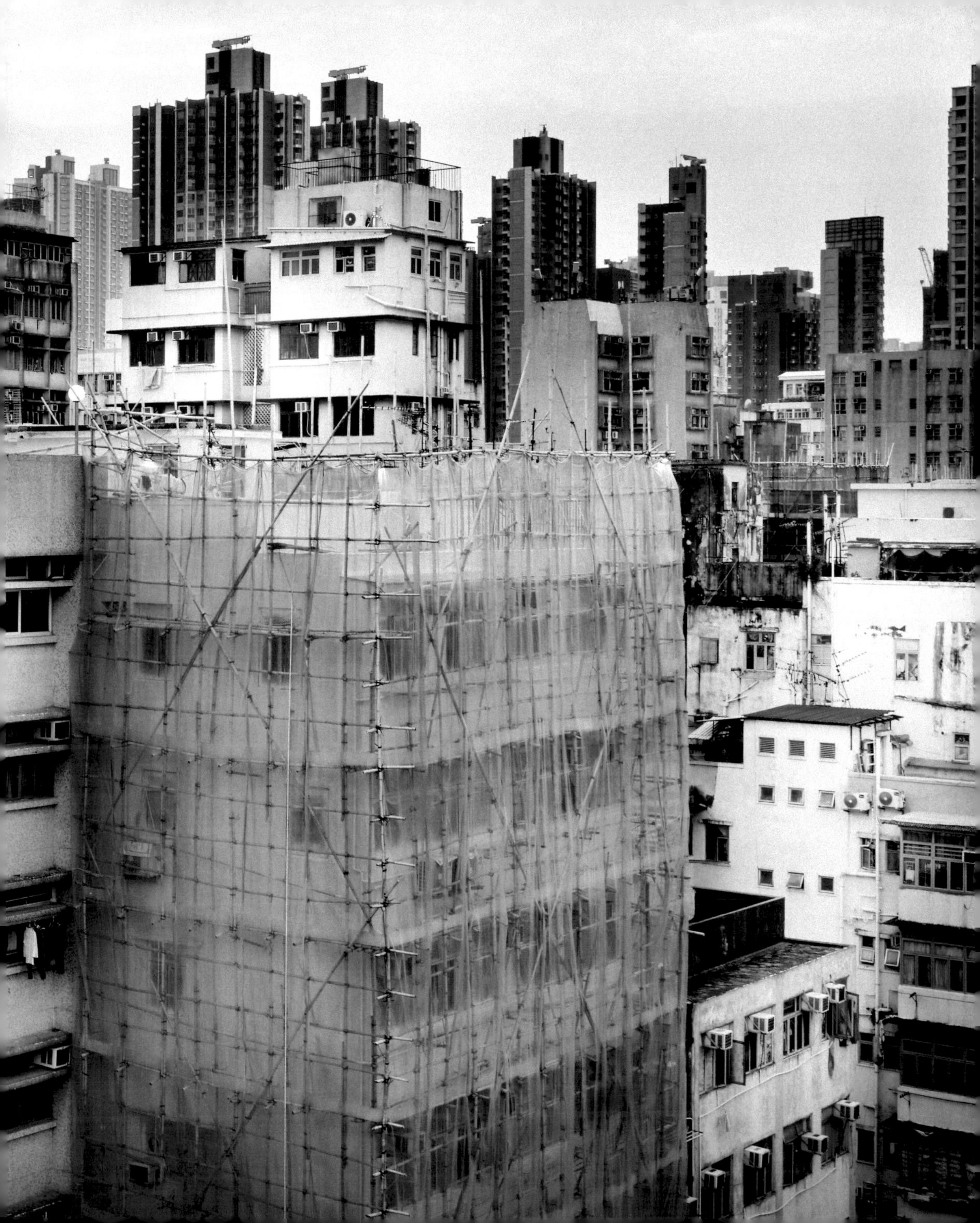

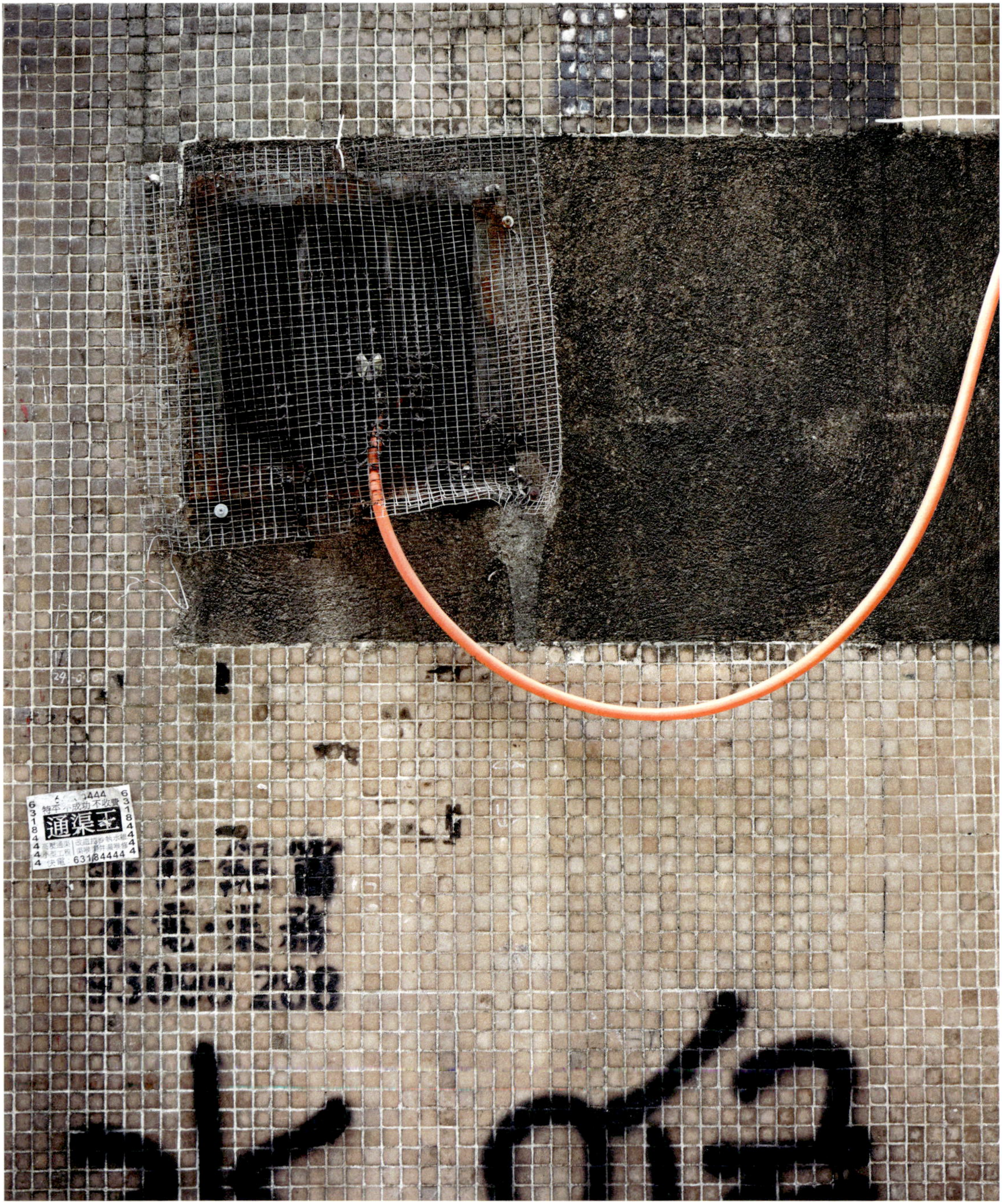

不成功 不收費
通渠
63184444

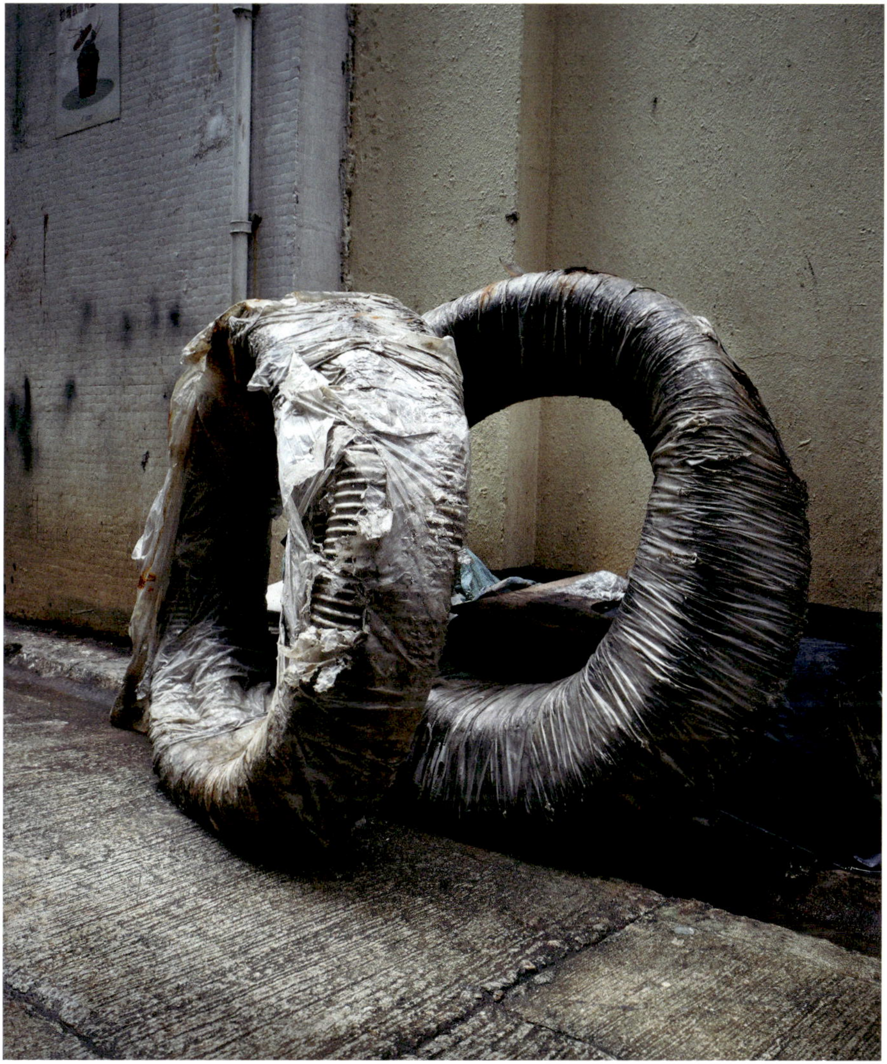

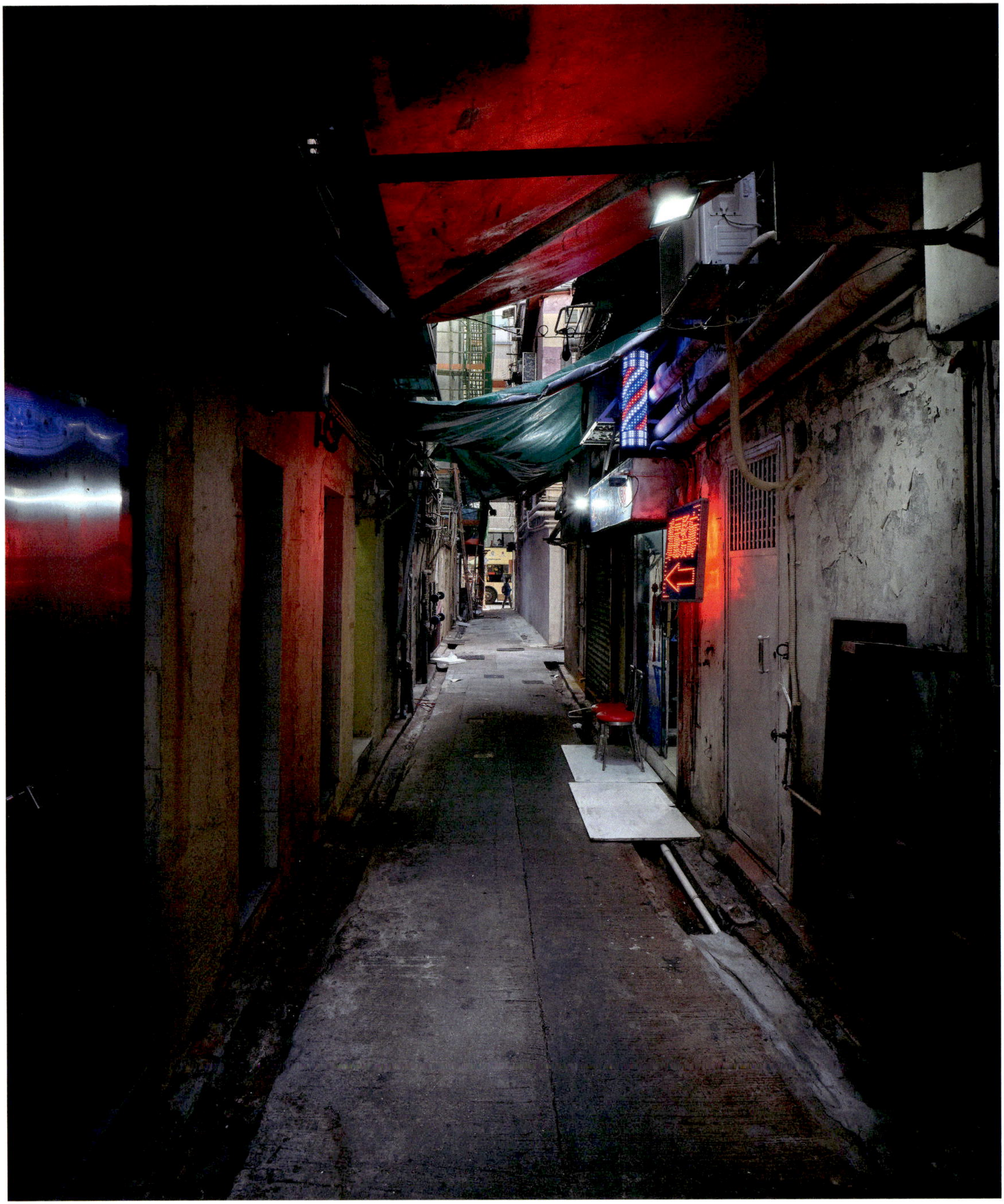

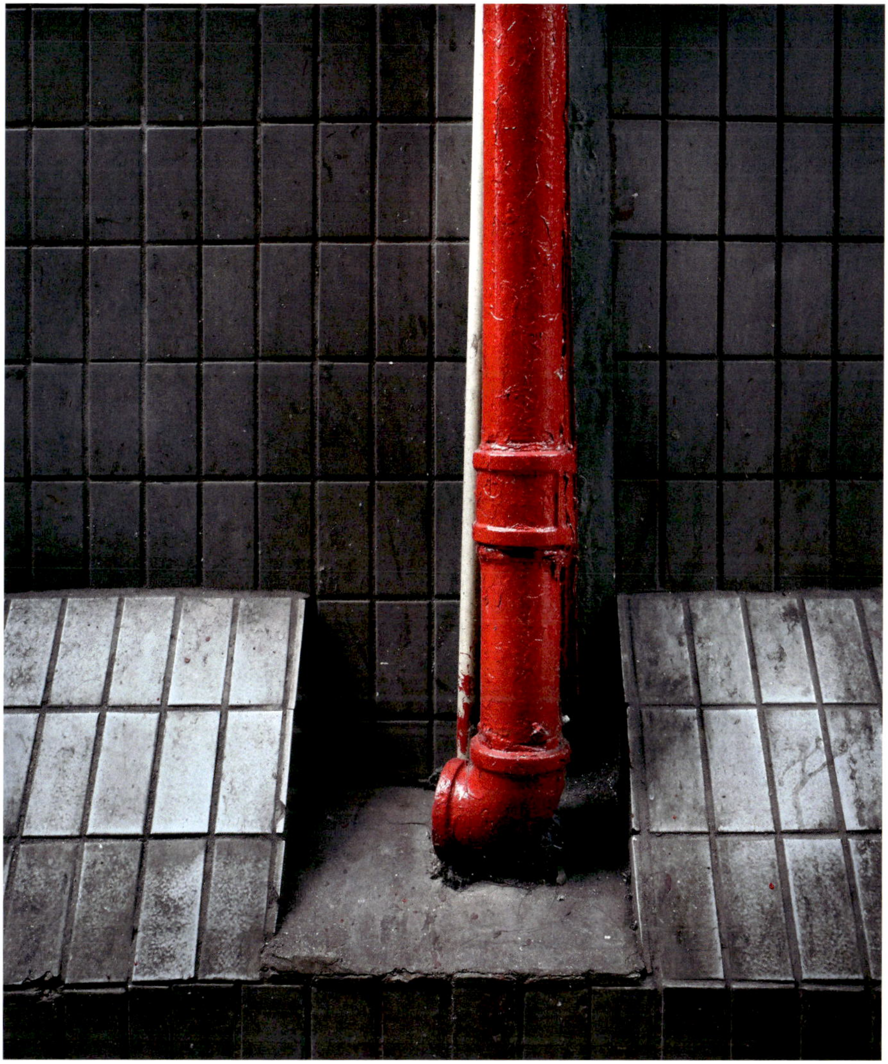

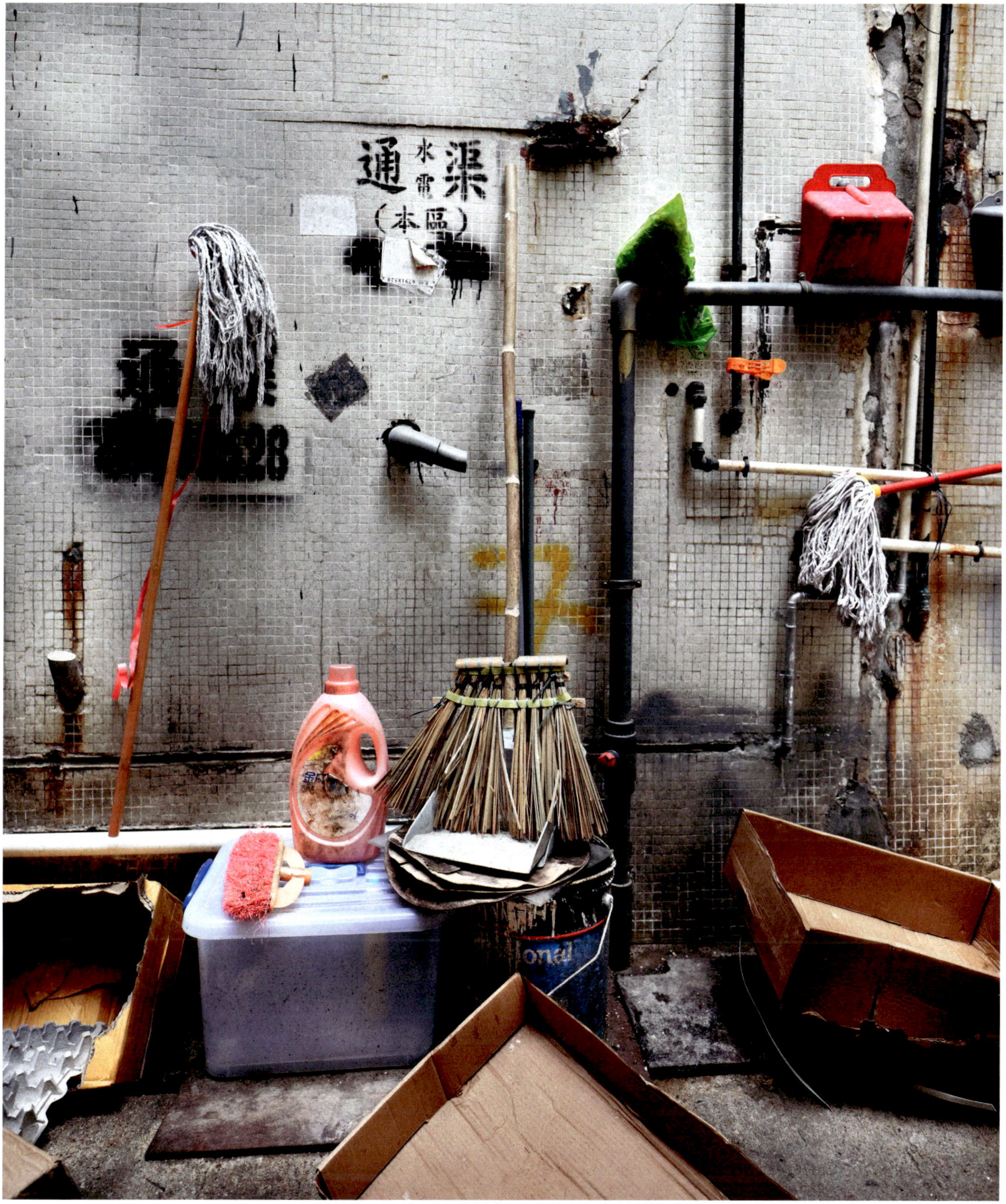
通 水電 渠
(本區)

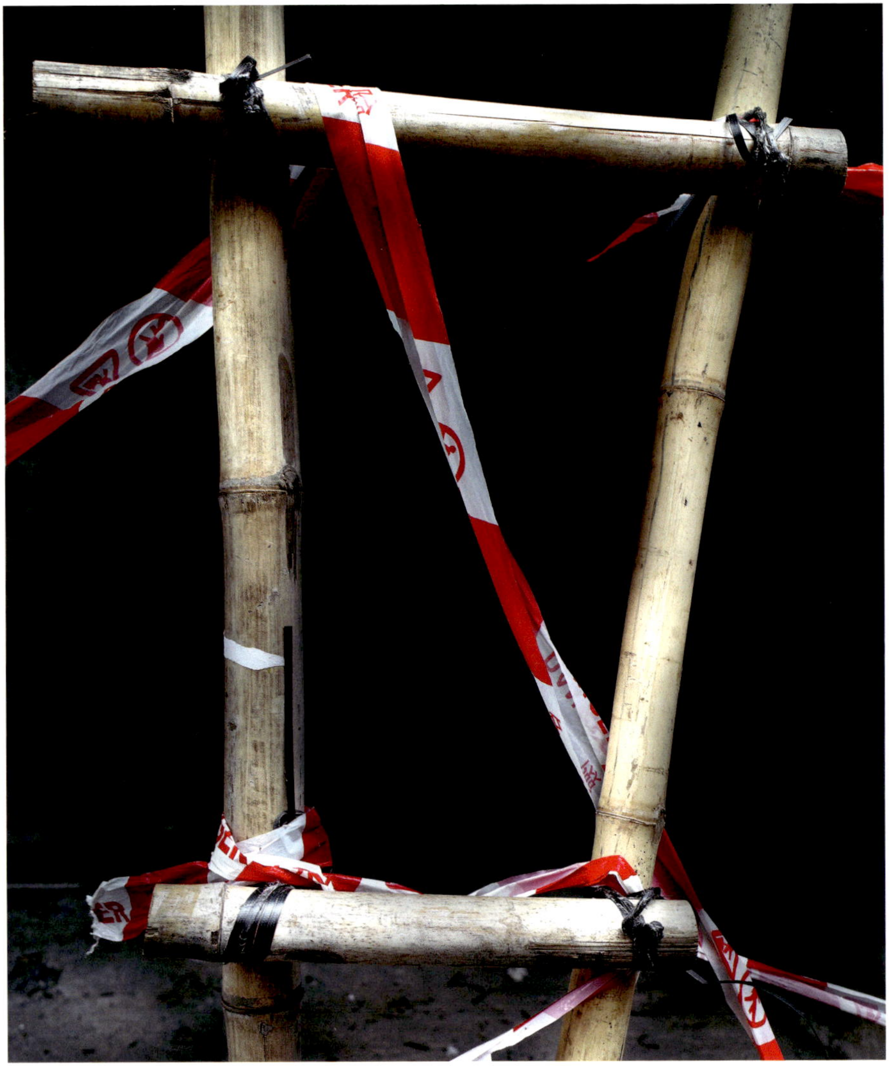

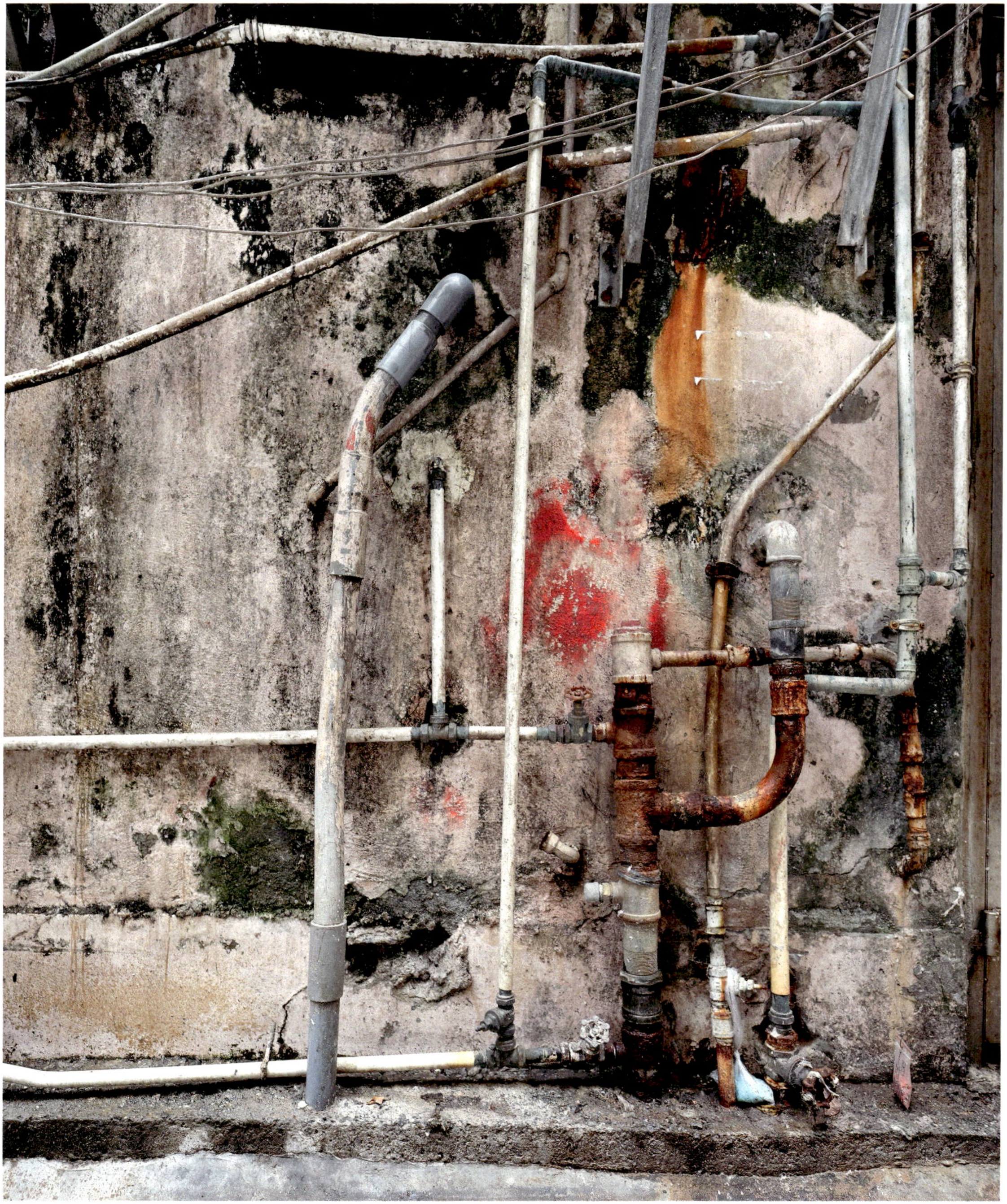

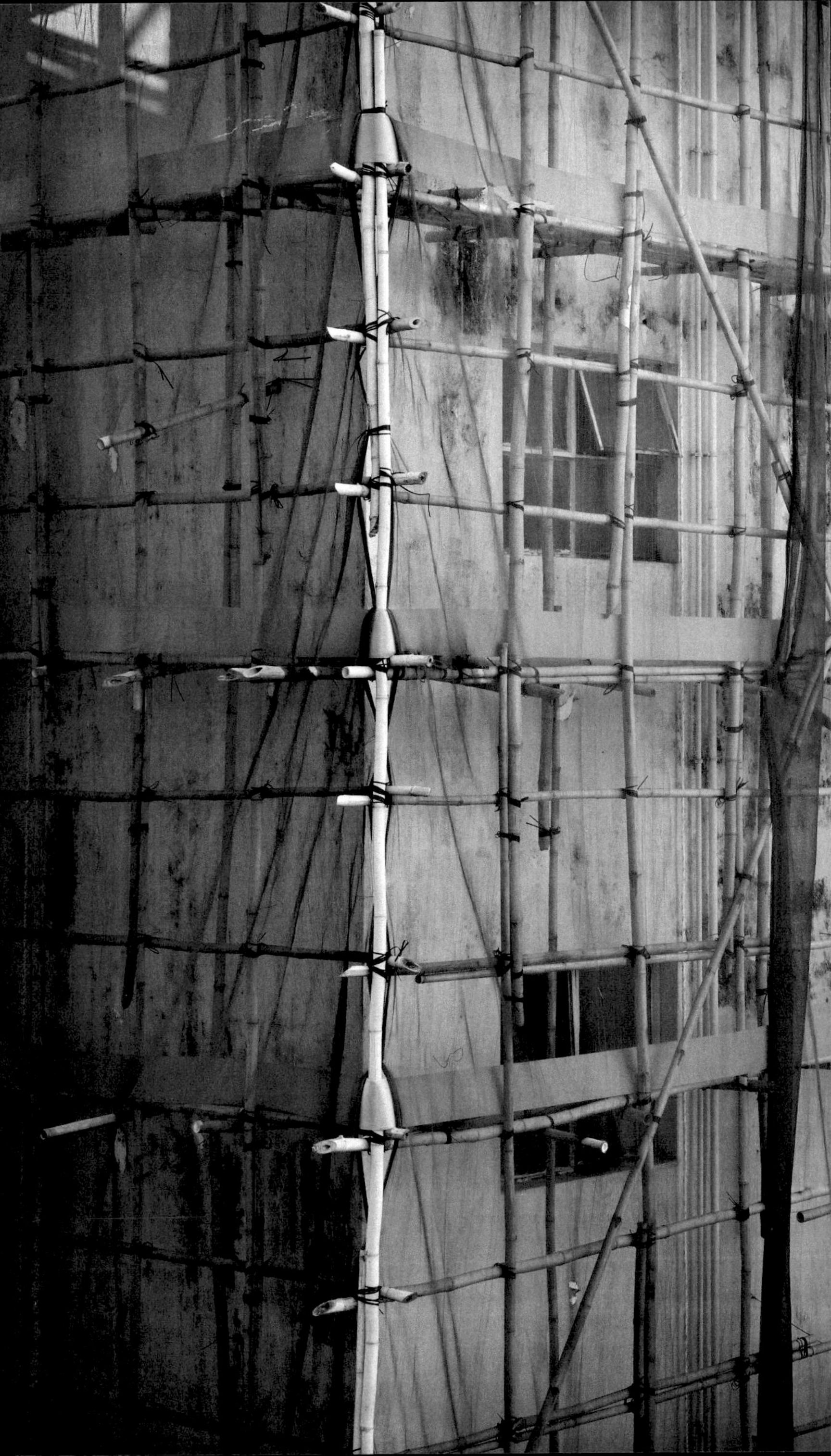

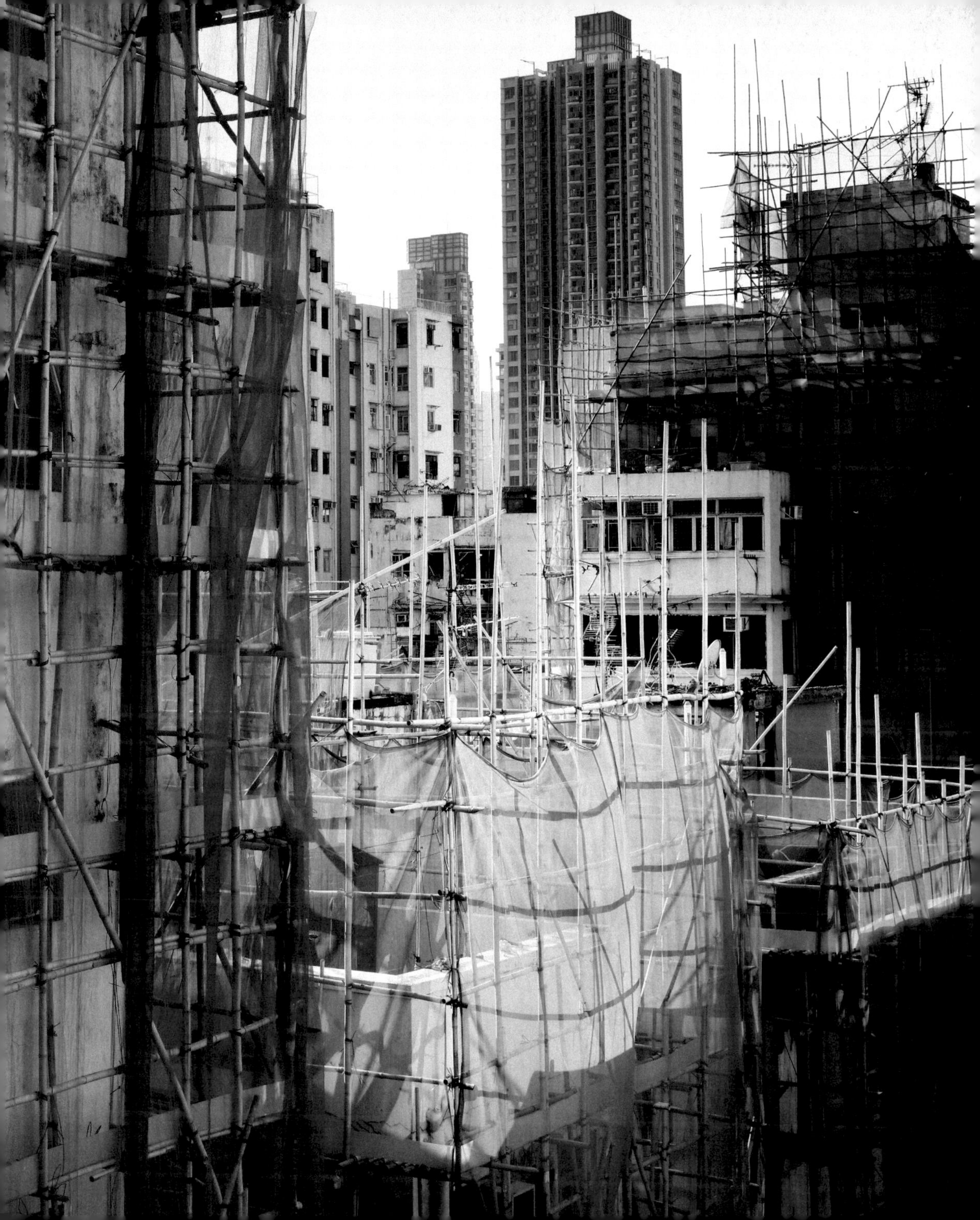

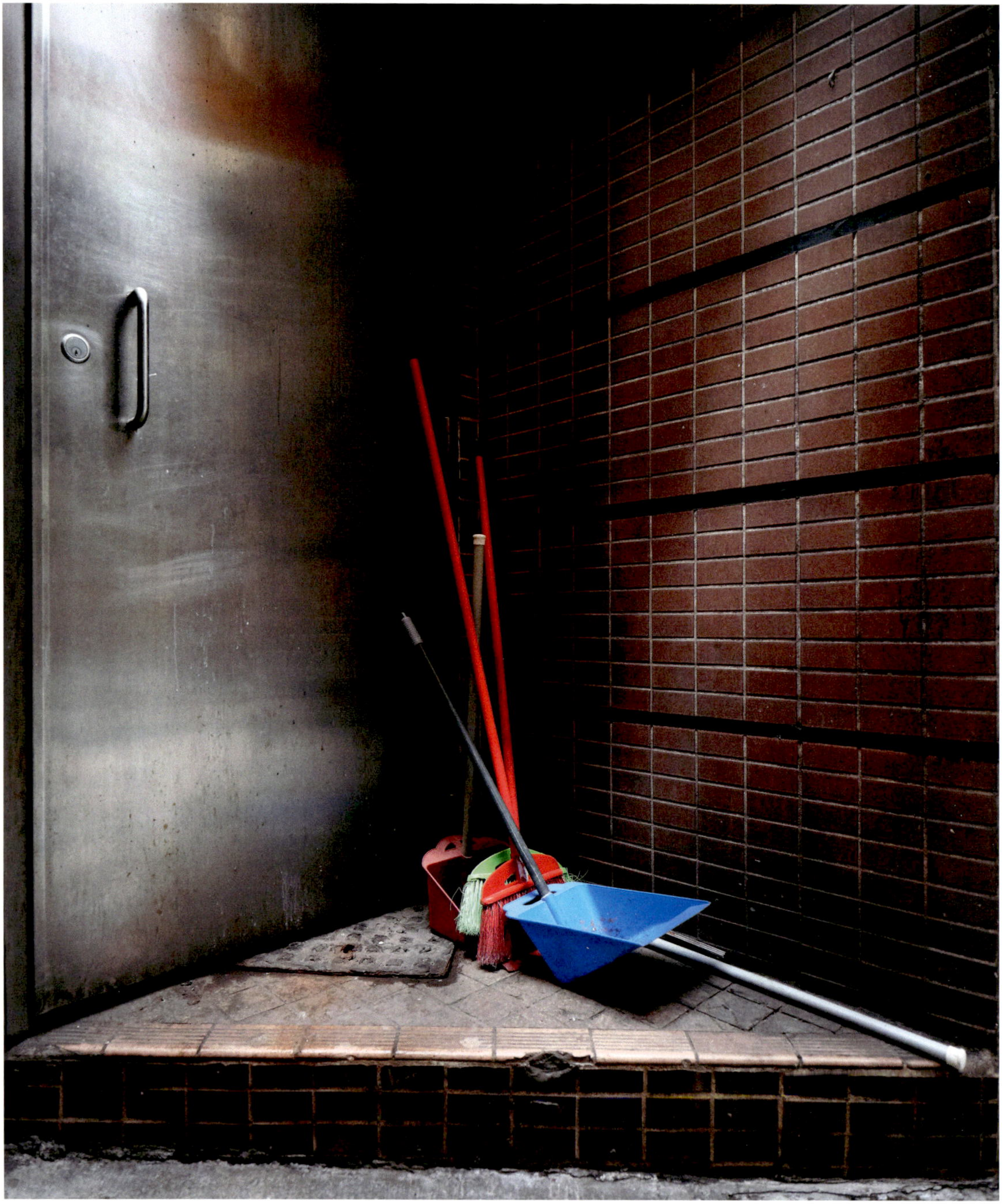

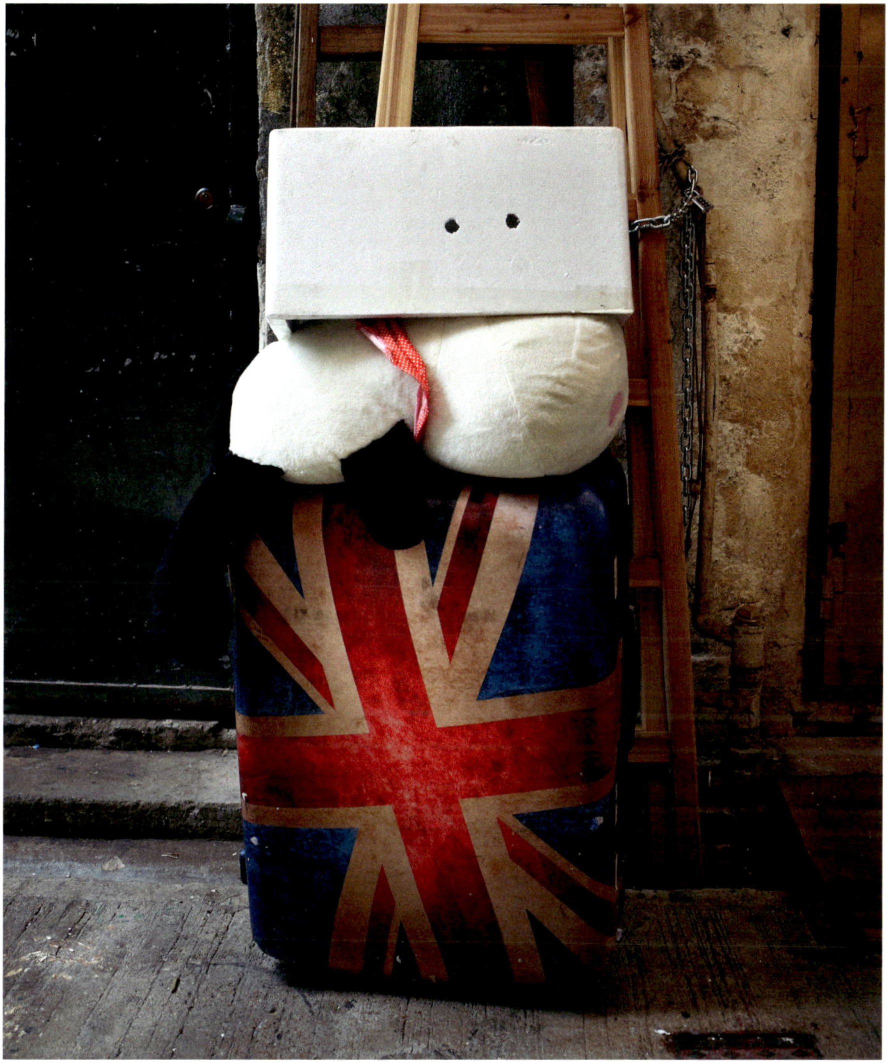

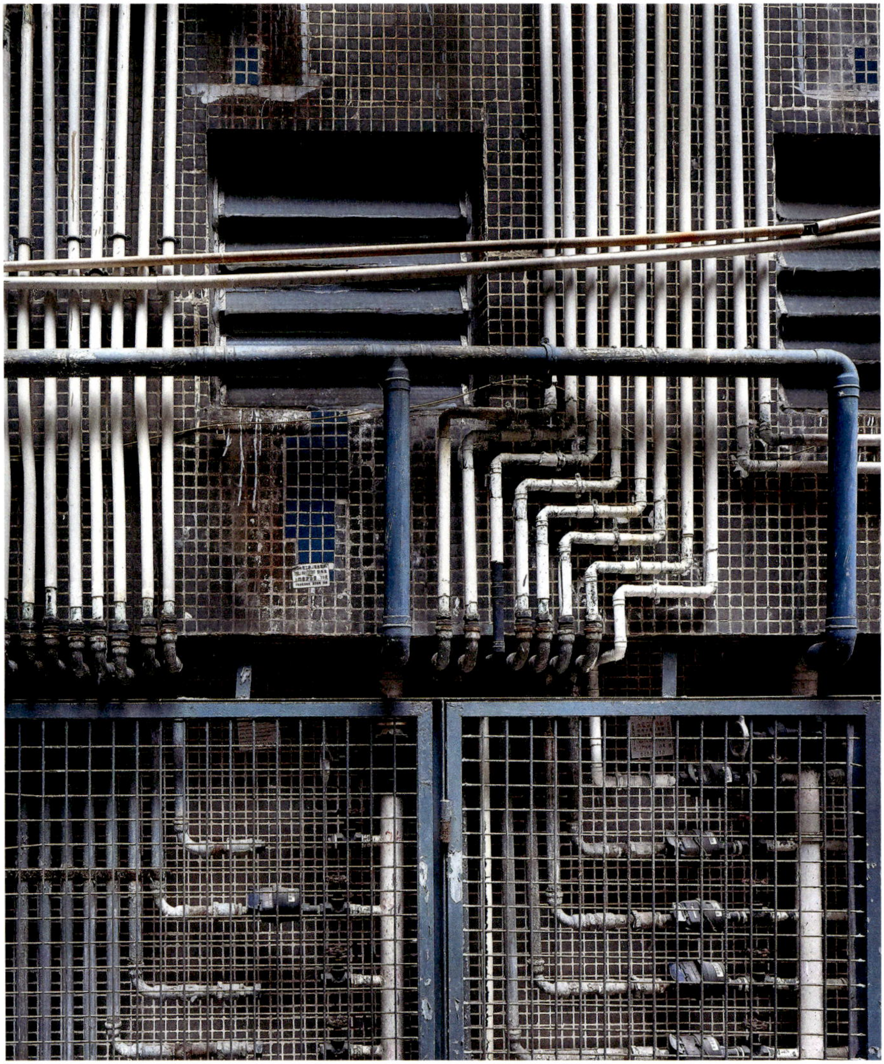

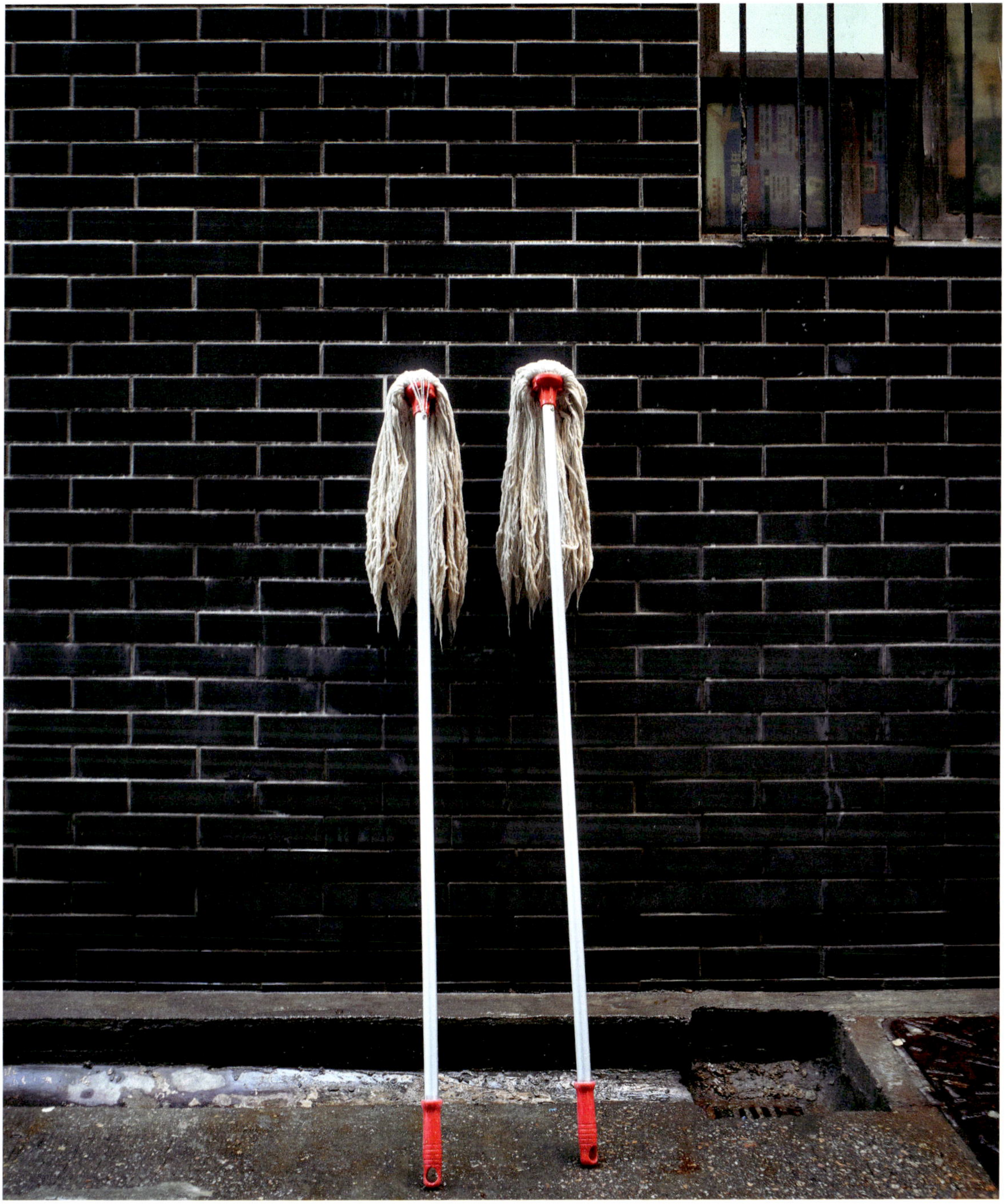

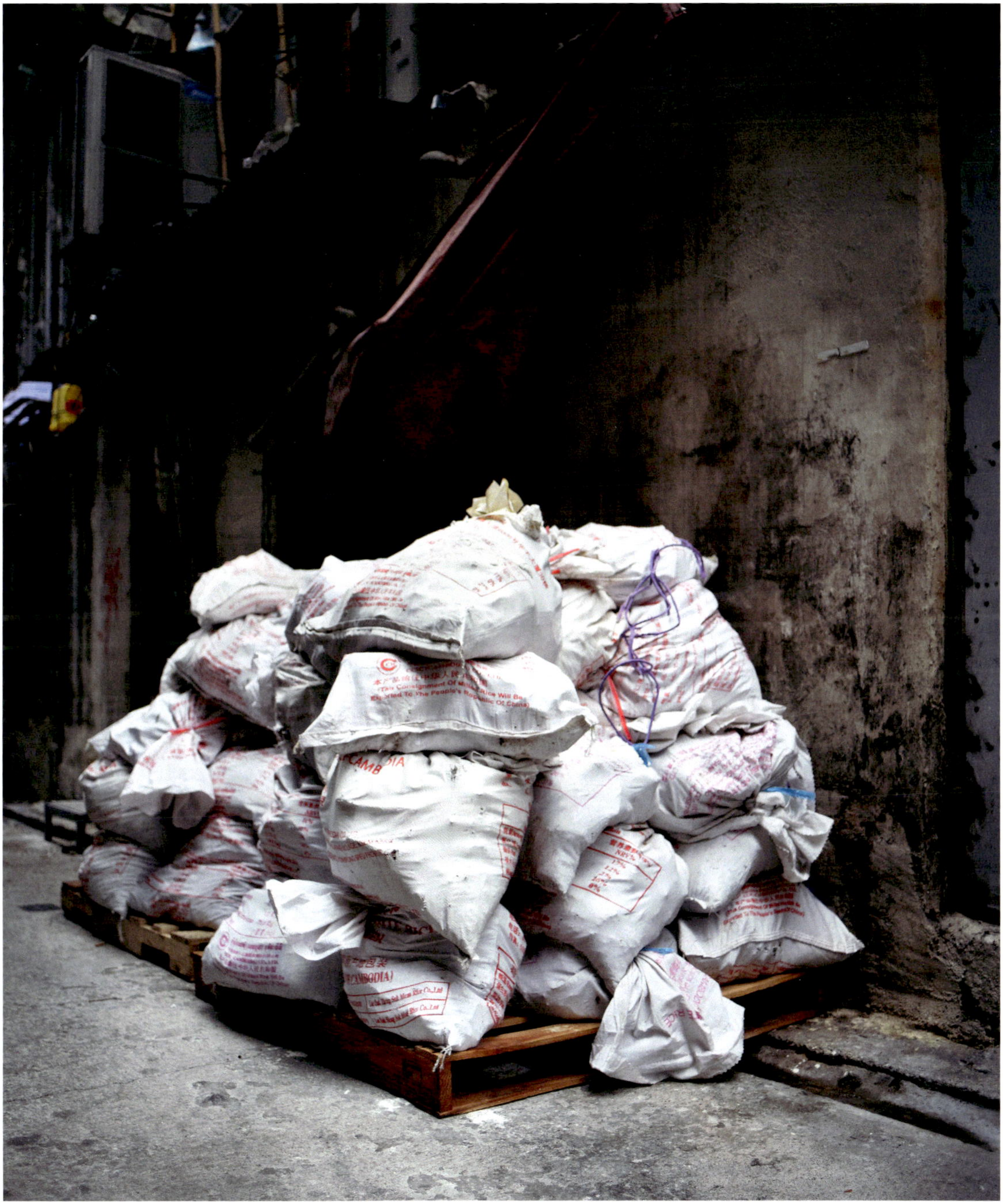
(CAMBODIA)

## Matthias Forster

Matthias Forster is interested in experimenting and moving between the different fields of photography and fine art. His visual language is characterised by clarity, originality and playfulness in the use of light, form and colour. As a curious person, he does not follow a clear concept, but rather his intuition. In his work he is particularly interested in the traces and legacies of mankind and the tension between chaos and order. With his keen observations, he visualises the everyday that is often overlooked.

After studying architecture, many years of experience in an established architecture firm and various travels, he completed his photography studies at the MAZ. Institut für Journalismus und Kommunikation in Lucerne in 2018 and has since been working as a freelance artist with a focus on independent photographic projects.

## Acknowledgements

After numerous visits and great enthusiasm for the metropolis of Hong Kong, the photos for the book were taken in 2019, 2020 and 2024.

In making the first selection of images, Alexa Becker laid the groundwork and contributed considerably to setting the overall epic tone of my pictorial language. A big thank you to the passionate book designer Hannah Feldmeier, who skilfully brought the book to its final, fitting form. Thanks to Uli Sigg, I was able to win Alberto Gerosa as the author of the text for this book. Alberto was immediately enthusiastic about the work, and I was able to meet him in person in Hong Kong in 2024. Alberto has lived in Sham Shui Po and since 2013 he has been transforming an alley into an open air art museum (Thy Lane Museum) around the clock and is very familiar with the subject. Many thanks to Alberto, who created a perfect written counterpart to my visual language. Thanks to copyeditor Anna E. Wilkens, every sentence and comma is just right. Jan Scheffler of professional prints made sure the images had the right colours and the right look for printing. DZA Druckerei ensured the beautiful print result. Thanks to Kerber Verlag, my publisher, I was able to make the book and design it the way I wanted. I would also like to thank all the many supporters not mentioned by name for their help.

Last but not least, I would like to thank my parents and my friends, especially Mathias, Michael, Peter, Boris, and my wife Luzia, without whose constant support my work would not be what it is.

Alberto Gerosa Volontè
contributed the texts
*Morning* (p. 21), *Afternoon* (p. 51),
and *Night* (p. 63).

**Photography**
Matthias Forster

**Texts**
Matthias Forster
Alberto Gerosa Volontè

**Image Editing and Consulting**
Alexa Becker

**Copyediting**
Anna E. Wilkens

**Graphic Design and Concept**
Hannah Feldmeier

**Lithography**
prints professional / Jan Scheffler

**Production**
Jens Bartneck / Kerber Verlag

**Project Management**
Lily von Wild / Kerber Verlag

**Printing and Binding**
DZA Druckerei zu Altenburg GmbH

**Paper**
Condat matt Périgord 150 g/m2

Kerber Verlag
Detmolder Straße 60
33604 Bielefeld
Germany
+49 521 950 08 10
+49 521 950 08 88 (F)
info@kerberverlag.com
kerberverlag.com

**Kerber publications are distributed worldwide:**

ACC Art Books
Sandy Lane
Old Martlesham
Woodbridge, IP12 4SD
UK
+44 1394 38 99 50
+44 1394 38 99 99 (F)
uksales@accartbooks.com
accartbooks.com

Artbook | D.A.P.
75 Broad Street, Suite 630
New York, NY 10004
USA
+1 (212) 627-1999
+1 (212) 627-9484 (F)
orders@dapinc.com
artbook.com

AVA Verlagsauslieferung AG
Centralweg 16
8910 Affoltern am Albis
Switzerland
+41 44 762 42 50
+41 44 762 42 10 (F)
avainfo@ava.ch

Zeitfracht Medien GmbH
Distribution
Germany
+49 711 7860 2254
service.zeitfracht.de

The Deutsche Nationalbibliothek lists this publication in the Deutsche Nationalbibliografie: dnb.de.



ISBN 978-3-7356-0989-2

www.kerberverlag.com

Printed in Germany